Learning about Writing

B

Language in Education
Series Editor
Michael Stubbs

Language is central to education. Yet very little writing about language is presented in a way that is suitable for teachers to help and guide them in their classroom practice. This series aims to explore in a non-technical way, aspects of language immediately relevant to practising and trainee teachers.

Learning about Writing: The Early Years
Pam Czerniewska

Teaching Grammar: A Guide for the National Curriculum
Richard Hudson

Learning about Writing
The Early Years

PAM CZERNIEWSKA

BLACKWELL
Oxford UK & Cambridge USA

Copyright © Pam Czerniewska

The right of Pam Czerniewska to be identified as author of this work has been
asserted in accordance with the Copyright, Designs and Patents Act 1988.

First published 1992
First published in USA 1992

Blackwell Publishers
108 Cowley Road, Oxford, OX4 1JF, UK

Three Cambridge Center
Cambridge, Massachusetts 02142, USA

British Library Cataloguing in Publication Data
A CIP catalogue record for this book is available from the British Library.

Library of Congress Cataloging in Publication Data
Czerniewska, Pam.
    Learning about writing: the early years / Pam Czerniewska.
        p. cm. — (Language in education)
    Includes bibliographical references and index.
    ISBN 0-631-16962-8. — ISBN 0-631-16963-6 (pbk.)
    1. English language—Composition and exercises—Study and teaching
(Elementary) I. Title. II. Series.
LB1576.C97 1992
372.6'23044—dc20   91-3818
                                                                      CIP

Typeset in 11 on 13 pt Palatino
by Photo·graphics, Honiton, Devon
Printed in Great Britain by Biddles Ltd, Guildford

This book is printed on acid-free paper.

Contents

Preface

This series contains short books on language in education, on topics where practical knowledge is urgently needed in schools.

The books aim to help with daily practice in schools and classrooms in principled ways. They should be of interest to practising teachers and student teachers, to teacher trainers, advisers and inspectors, and to those involved in educational administration, at the level of head of department or head of school, or in local education authorities.

The books follow several important guidelines:

- their main purpose is to make knowledge about language accessible to those who need it.
- they therefore avoid jargon and presuppose no knowledge at all about linguistics
- they are not, in fact, books about linguistics but books about language, informed by current linguistic thinking
- they contain large numbers of examples, which, as far as possible, are taken from real data, such as children's written work, transcripts of classroom talk and pupils' school textbooks
- they discuss topics which teachers and parents themselves think are important: What *is* grammar and why doesn't it seem to be taught these days? How do children learn to write? Why can't some children learn to spell? What is normal and abnormal in language

development? Why is there so much debate about English teaching? . . .

A great deal of knowledge has been gained about many linguistic topics which are important in education. For practical purposes, such knowledge can be accepted as widely agreed and factual – at least it is the best which we have available in areas where it is badly needed by teachers, advisors and administrators. However, this knowledge is often not in an appropriate form: it is often in journal articles or in relatively technical books. It is therefore the responsibility of linguists to present it to teachers, clearly and in an accessible form. If this is not done then practical decisions will still be taken by individual teachers and others – but possibly uninformed by the best in current thinking about language in education.

There have recently been very large changes in the British education system, particularly centred on the Education Reform Act and the National Curriculum. In a longer term perspective, the changes which this legislation has brought about are part of a long struggle around the forms and purposes of education. But debates about teaching English as a mother tongue and teaching foreign languages have certainly been very sharp in recent years. And there is no doubt that 'knowledge about language' has been given particular prominence (and has received a great deal of publicity in the mass media) via the curriculum proposals for English and modern languages. 'Standard English' and related topics carry a heavy symbolic load, and much of the discussion, sometimes fuelled by statements by prominent politicians and other public figures, has been confused and even hysterical. An aim of this series is to encourage considered and rational debate in an area where deeply felt emotions are often at stake.

The books in the series have been written with British teachers in mind, though the issues they discuss are clearly also of relevance in other countries. Due to rapid changes in the school system, British teachers are currently under considerable pressures, and are under particular pressures in areas of the curriculum which concern language.

The aim, then, is to provide critical studies of aspects of language which are important to professional practice: to identify problems and help to solve them with reference to the best current knowledge about language. The books are not therefore primarily conceived as theoretical contributions. However, if linguists seriously think about language as it is used in schools and classrooms, this inevitably leads to new insights, and such studies of language in use may well raise theoretical problems of fundamental interest to linguists.

This book by Pam Czerniewska tackles a problem which is of central concern to parents and teachers: how children learn to use written language. Czerniewska is very well qualified indeed to discuss this question. She has developed courses on language for teachers at the Open University, she has directed an adult literacy project in New York, and more recently she has directed the British National Writing Project, which was very influential for individual teachers and also had considerable influence on the formation of the National Curriculum in English. This book is full of examples of children's work which was collected and analysed during the project, and it provides a clear and principled account of some of the new thinking about how children learn to write.

Series editor, Michael Stubbs

Acknowledgements

'Language is more than how it describes itself, it connects everything and everybody together; in every sentence there is a sense of our collaborative dialogue.' Margaret Spencer spoke these words in her farewell lecture at the London Institute of Education. They express for me the debt I owe to all the people whose words helped me to write this book.

I would like to name a few of the individuals with whom I have had many conversations and debates about writing and whose thoughts have constantly challenged my own. My thanks, in particular, to Eve Bearne, Barbara Grayson, John Richmond, Jeremy Tafler and Judy Phillips with whom, as colleagues on the National Writing Project, I spent some very exciting years working with teachers around the country. Special thanks, too, to Janet Maybin, Neil Mercer and Janet White whose knowledge about literacy and education significantly informed my own.

Sadly, I cannot begin to name all the teachers who have assisted my thinking by welcoming me into their classrooms and reflecting on their experiences. Some are quoted in this book; many others will, I hope, hear themselves in the conclusions reached.

Finally, I would like to thank my family for their endurance while I worked through the various drafts of this book.

Publisher's Note

Every effort has been made to trace all copyright holders, but if any has been inadvertently overlooked the publishers will be pleased to make the necessary arrangements at the first opportunity.

Introduction

The original idea for this book was to bring together thoughts about young children's writing development based on my observations of and work in primary school classrooms; my conversations with teachers, parents and children about writing and my discussions with researchers about models of writing development. It would be a synthesis of classroom practices that I had learned about and helped to develop largely through my work with the National Writing Project, 1985–9. It was to be a celebration of the excellent activities that make up the primary writing curriculum at its best.

But while my starting point was classroom practice, I also wanted to provide a theoretical framework within which curriculum developments could be placed and evaluated. This involved me in a process of critical reflection in which I began asking myself awkward questions about literacy, learning and education. I felt that to justify any judgements I might reach about what makes 'good' practice, I needed to think through issues such as the status of literacy in our society; how we think children learn; how schools define literacy; and whether the definition is broad enough to encompass the wide variety of literacy practices used by different social groups.

Thus, my story of writing development in the early years begins outside the classroom with some reflections on the relationships between literacy and culture. The picture that emerges from the research is that literacy cannot be encompassed by a single definition, neither can it be reduced to a set of skills. Writing development involves more than the acquisition of handwriting, spelling rules and knowledge of various forms of writing. Writing, like other aspects of language, is a social process, something that happens in different ways in different contexts and in different cultural groups.

When children learn to write, they learn more than the *system* of writing. They learn about the *social practices* of language: for example, that shopping lists can be jointly written by family members; that parents must not be disturbed when filling in important forms; or that writing should be on paper not on walls. Children learn, too, the cultural values of different types of writing: for example, that some notes are scribbled then thrown away; that some writing is carefully kept; or that some writing is to be learned by rote. What each child learns about writing will vary among social groups. For some groups, writing plays a central role in daily lives; for others, writing has a peripheral role. Some see writing as an act that is best done collaboratively, with a lot of accompanying talk; others see writing as a predominantly solitary and private event.

To start with a social perspective on literacy involves going beyond the linguistic characteristics of writing, and tries to take into account the cultural values and social characteristics of the participants. It looks at, to quote Cook-Gumperz, 'processes by which literacy is constructed in everyday life through interactional exchanges and the negotiation of meaning in many different contexts' (1986, p. 2). Applying this perspective to the classroom, questions emerge about the ways in which schools have defined the writing task. One significant concern raised by an analysis of the ways schools have constructed literacy is the extent to which the multiplicity of values and consequences of different literacy practices is recognized and explored.

Alongside general issues about literacy come important questions about learners and learning. What models of learning do we hold as we develop the writing curriculum? How is the child viewed? The past few years have seen a dramatic change in the way in which the process of learning to write has been described. The child is seen as someone who enters school with a wealth of knowledge about literacy practices. This has not been learned in a passive way. Rather, the child has engaged actively in working out how writing is organized, how it is used and how it is valued. The child will have developed her own theories about writing, revising these a number of times as her knowledge develops. With an understanding of the child's role in the learning process, we can begin to talk about ways of organizing the writing environment and ways of assessing development.

Furthermore, the child's knowledge about writing will have developed through her interactions with parents, teachers and peers. Writing can thus be seen as a joint construction of adult and child. It is not enough to think about the nature of the writing system and the nature of the learning process in order to formulate a writing policy. We need also to consider how the writing tasks are negotiated between the pupils and the teacher. This raises major issues such as what types of writing are being valued by teachers? How do different groups of children (e.g. boys and girls) respond to particular writing tasks? What expectations do teachers hold for different children's development?

To begin this book with three chapters on the nature of literacy and of learning may seem to take rather a long way round to reach the primary classroom. But I hope that the broader perspective offered helps to place current curriculum innovations in their social context and enables us to evaluate future fashions in terms of their underlying views of literacy and learning. The nature of writers and writing has been defined in different ways by each new wave of curriculum ideas for writing. But each new writing model builds on those that have come before. What looks at first like a radical shift in thinking, often turns out to share the same fundamental assumptions of existing practice. In describing a few examples of current practice, I have tried to identify the main ideas about writing and about learning on which different activities are based. In this way, I hope that the development of the writing curriculum can build on the strengths of past and current experiences.

1

Literacy in Communities and Classrooms

A ten-year-old, when asked whether he enjoyed writing, answered 'I like writing because if we didn't write in school we would have nothing to do all day.'

Writing is a central activity of the school curriculum. This is not surprising given the high value placed on literacy in Western society. The dominant position given to writing is not simply because it is seen as a useful skill to have, but because writing represents a special kind of learning, one that provides access to higher intellectual levels and to better work prospects. Its privileged status can be recognized in the way that writing is regarded, in both the teachers' and the pupils' minds, as the best way of representing learning. Writing predominates over talk as the proof that learning has taken place and the highest awards go to those who can achieve well on written assessments. Writing and reading are among the major aspects of the child's education that parents are anxious about, a fact well testified by the abundance of articles in popular magazines that ostensibly help parents prepare their child for literacy. Adults who cannot write are generally considered by themselves and by others as intellectually inferior. And when the state of education is being addressed by media or politicians, the yardstick used is usually the level of literacy acquired by pupils.

The message that literacy is important is one that is learned by children from a very young age. For example, in surveys of pupils' perceptions of writing (e.g. National Writing Project, 1990b), children of all ages who are asked why they should learn to write mention that writing is a sign of intellectual achievement: 'without writing people would think you are stupid.' They also think that writing helps you cope with the demands of later life: 'you need it to get a job . . . to fill in forms . . . when you go to big school.' Beneath these claims lies a tradition of thinking which has elevated literacy to its very high status. As Paul Gee puts it:

As the final products of nearly four thousand years of an alphabetic literacy, we all tend to believe strongly in the powerful and redeeming effects of literacy, especially in times of complex social and economic crises. (Gee, 1988, p. 196)

Literacy frequently bears the responsibility for social and intellectual development. Greater emphasis on literacy is often seen as the means of preventing educational failure. When children have been labelled as educationally disadvantaged, the missing ingredient is commonly thought to be 'literacy'. Literacy means more than the ability to read and write, it means being able to demonstrate knowledge in particular, socially approved ways. In other words, literacy is a socially constructed phenomenon that represents the key to success, to jobs and to intellectual achievements.

As the main purpose of this book is to look at how children learn to write and how schools can support this development, it seems appropriate to begin with some general questions about literacy. Is its high status deserved: does literacy itself lead to new intellectual heights, better jobs, to achievement in 'big school'? And more than this, is the model of literacy promoted by schools broad enough to represent the range of literacy practices available in the community? Many argue that schools have defined literacy as a special and narrow range of practices. One possible consequence of such a definition is that some literacy practices used in the community may come to be seen as sociolinguistic deficits, as 'the cause and product of the inability to use literate reasoning' (Cook-Gumperz, 1986, p. 43). Questions about what schools mean by literacy may reveal a social selection process wherein only certain groups have full access to literacy and its associated intellectual and economic fortunes.

Literate traditions

'A person who writes clearly thinks clearly' . . . 'I need to be able to write it down in order to understand it.' These are familiar expressions which underlie a prevailing view that literacy holds a key to our thinking processes. They are ones that are to be found in the conclusions of scientists from a range of disciplines from anthropology to psychology. Vygotsky (1978), for example, discussed the different psychological functions involved in writing compared with talk and attributed a different cognitive status to the written form. Others, working along Piagetian lines, have suggested that literacy may be the key factor to higher reasoning abilities. Donaldson, for instance, speculates:

Thus it turns out that those very features of the written word which encourage awareness of language may also encourage awareness of one's own thinking and be relevant to the development of intellectual self-control, with incalculable consequences for the development of the kinds of thinking which are characteristic of logic, mathematics and the sciences. (Donaldson, 1978, p. 95)

Others have gone further and seen the invention of writing systems as the big breakthrough in the development of civilization. Goody (1977) sees the development and spread of literacy as a central factor in explaining how modes of thought and cultural organization change over time. Reading and writing, he argues, are necessary prerequisites for higher forms of reasoning and logic and for the development of political systems. Gee summarizes Goody's conclusions:

Goody relates the development of writing to the growth of individualism, the growth of bureaucracy and of more depersonalised and more abstract systems of government, as well as the development of the abstract thought and syllogistic reasoning that culminate in modern science. Goody sees the acquisition of writing as effectively transforming the nature of both cognitive and social processes. (Gee, 1986)

The implication of such claims is that those from less-literate communities are in some sense intellectually inferior, and need to acquire literacy in order to engage in more technologically advanced activities. Such claims receive support from the lower performance of less-literate groups on various psychological tests of cognitive ability.

How well founded are the claims that literacy has important cognitive consequences, leading to a form of abstract reasoning necessary for coping with the demands of technological advances? The belief is certainly deep rooted, with practitioners and students often expressing the correlation between ability to read and write well and ability to cope with complex reasoning tasks and to hold positions of power.

Such a belief has not been without critics from the time that literacy became widespread. Plato, for instance, questioned the value of literacy when he attacked writing for leading to a deterioration of memory (no need now for people to remember epic poems) and for providing people with crutches that would allow them to quote knowledge that they had not reflected on and defended themselves. In an extract of dialogue from Plato's *Phaedrus* (Rowe, 1986, quoted in Gee, 1988), Socrates makes two interrelated charges against writing: that it cannot defend itself and that it cannot stand up to questioning:

Socrates: . . . I think writing has this strange feature, which makes it like painting. The offspring of painting stand there as if alive, but if you ask them something, they preserve a quite solemn silence. Similarly with written words: you might think that they spoke as if they had some thought in their heads, but if you ever ask them about any of the things they say out of a desire to learn, they point to just one thing, the same thing each time. And when once it is written, every composition is trundled about everywhere in the same way, in the presence both of those who know about the subject and of those who have nothing at all to do with it, and it does not know how to address those it should address and not those it should not. When it is ill-treated and unjustly abused, it always needs its father to help it; for it is incapable of defending or helping itself. (Rowe, 1986, p. 275, quoted in Gee, 1988, p. 197)

But, despite Plato's warnings, writing has become a central

aspect of language use, and universal literacy has become an increasingly important goal. Its spread has been associated with various changes in its value. For example, in the nineteenth century, literacy was strongly linked with moral worth. Later, links strengthened between literacy and economic success and literacy and reasoning powers. In the context of education, it is useful to explore further the correlations claimed between literacy and cognitive abilities.

A rather different line of attack from Plato's, questions whether the higher performance of literate people on particular reasoning tasks reflects a general increase in intellectual ability. Perhaps it is simply that the type of literacy taught in schools results in a few specific cognitive skills, which are different but not necessarily more advanced than the skills exhibited through talk and through other types of non-school literacy. The cognitive skills tested in comparisons of literate and less-literate groups may reflect a limited range of intellectual abilities learned in schools rather than some general reasoning powers.

Some argue (e.g. Street, 1984) that school literacy covers only a narrow range of literacy practices. In schools, writing is largely restricted to the expository or essay-type text in which knowledge is displayed and can be analysed for its structure and logicality. In addition, there is the fostering of story-writing in which the text follows a prescribed structure and can be judged according to how well it has been crafted. Models of writing development commonly see progress in terms of children's control over story and essay-type writing. One possible consequence of this weighting is that other writing, particularly that done outside the school, is ignored or given a lower status. A one-sided view of writing is created which ignores the many values and consequences of other literacy practices.

In order to explore whether conclusions about the cognitive effects of literacy derive from a narrow view of literacy from a particular cultural context, Scribner and Cole (1981) carried out comparative research among the Vai, a group of people in north-west Liberia. The Vai have a unique set of literacies which means that school and literacy are not necessarily connected. There are three scripts: Vai, Arabic and English, each with their own, but overlapping, functions. Vai is used mainly for personal letters and commercial purposes, though also for records of clan histories and for stories. Most adult males are literate in Vai, having learned it not in school but with the help of a friend or relative. In addition, some are literate in Arabic in the sense that they have learned to read and write the Qu'ran. Teaching of Qu'ranic verses is largely through rote memorization and the majority are literate without understanding what the text says. The third literacy is English, the language used for administrative and political purposes. This form of writing is learned in government and mission schools located outside the community. Thus there are those Vai who have literacy but no schooling; those who have learned to write in school, and those who have no literacy. Furthermore, there are forms of literacy associated with very specific functions shared by only some of the population.

Scribner and Cole used a number of psychological measures to see whether literacy *per se* had an effect on performance in verbal reasoning tasks. They found that it was those literate in English, that is, the ones that had been to school, who performed better on tasks involving logical explanations, answers to hypothetical questions and various kinds of abstract reasoning: tasks which the researchers categorized as 'talking about' tasks. On other tasks, differences between groups seemed to be best explained by looking at the specific practices used by the group. So, for example, Arabic literates performed better on certain memory tasks; Vai literates were better at talking about Vai, its correct forms and its structure. The conclusion that can be drawn from this account is that claims for global consequences of literacy are not supported. What seems to be the case is that specific literacy practices enhance specific skills. Schools, where the display and analysis of decontextualized knowledge is practised, develop learners who are able to perform well on tasks requiring decontextualized skills. But there is no evidence that this is a general intellectual ability underpinning other abilities. As Scribner and Cole put it:

Nothing in our data would support the [view] that reading and writing entail 'cognitive restructurings' that control intellectual performance in all domains. Quite the contrary: the very specificity of the effects suggests that they may be closely tied to performance parameters of a limited set of tasks. . . . (Quoted in Mercer, 1988, p. 253)

The conclusion that can be reached from this unique piece of research is that literacy has been defined by schools to represent a particular set of language practices and a specific way of representing knowledge. There are other literacy practices outside school which have equally significant effects on our thinking. However, the schooling process may serve to exclude some groups from entry to education and from certain kinds of success. According to Scribner and Cole, 'The monolithic model of what writing is and what it leads to . . . appears in the light of comparative data to fail to give full justice to the multiplicity of values, uses and consequences which characterises writing as social practice' (Quoted in Mercer, 1988, p. 253).

Whose literacy?

The argument I am trying to develop here is that the concept we have of literacy as it is presented in schools is a culturally constructed one. Other literacies, i.e. ways of behaving with printed material, are practised and valued in other contexts or in other communities. How literacy is defined will change over time and differ among cultures. New ways of constructing literacy are particularly evident at times when technological innovations introduce new patterns of interaction with print. Electronic mail, Fax, television and so on have all created new patterns of writing. Furthermore, at a time when social and economic conditions are in upheaval, some of the former correlations of literacy with job prospects and positions of power no longer hold true, and values attributed to particular literacy practices have to be re-evaluated.

To discover more about the social practices of literacy, various ethnographic studies have been carried out. These studies involve researchers living in different communities, and collecting data from their daily lives to see 'where, when, how for whom and with what results are individuals in different social groups of today's highly industrialised society using reading and writing skills?' (Heath, 1982b, p. 93). The concern of such research is with language *events* used in different communities which are often very different from the types of language use available in schools.

Shirley Brice Heath, for example, made a major study in the American Piedmont Carolinas of three different communities which she called Trackton, Roadville and Maintown. Her main focus was on 'any occasion in which a piece of writing is integral to the nature of participants' interactions and their interpretive processes' (Heath, 1982b, p. 93). Thus the literacy events which she collected included reading letters, filling in forms, writing shopping lists and singing with a hymn book.

Her findings showed how children learn from their culture different means of using and making sense of print and different ways of relating their knowledge of the world through talk and writing. As she puts it, community cultures introduce children to different 'ways of taking' meaning from the environment around them (Heath, 1983, p. 49). Different literate traditions derive from varying patterns of interaction among adults and between children and adults during literacy events. Only some of the ways of taking from books that children learn will match the literate tradition established by schools; for many social groups there may be a mismatch and the children may well not succeed as a result.

A brief summary of Shirley Brice Heath's comparative study of book-reading habits (which does not do justice to the full account) will illustrate the different patterns of interaction and paths of development that she found in the three US communities.

The Maintown ways of taking will probably be the most familiar of the three to readers of this book. The child's environment is filled with print and with information derived from print. There are books and print-decorated friezes and there are also ornaments, clothes and toys based on characters from books. Reading activities from six months old encourage talk about book content: 'What's that? What's she doing there?

What colour is that ball?' and to relate book information to the child's own life: 'That's like your duck. Does your mummy do that?' Opportunities are always being found in the Maintown home for real events to be related to book events: 'Are you going to eat it all up "Owp" like the tiger who came to tea?' And the child is rewarded whenever she takes on a character from a book: 'Oh yes, you're just like Goldilocks eating everyone's porridge.' Children quickly learn that saying 'read a book mummy' is a sure way of getting mother's undivided attention, as is making up their own stories. Within this tradition, children are encouraged to suspend reality and tell stories which are not true. Many misdemeanours can be forgiven with the words 'but I'm just pretending like in the book.' As children get older book behaviour is accompanied by certain procedural rules such as 'I'm not going to go on reading unless you sit properly' and there are fewer interruptions of the reading with questions about the text. Heath notes how central books are to the Maintown homes and what authority they have over behaviour. Book-reading can interrupt almost any event and children's literature is a source of great fascination to the adults.

This way of taking from books, involving not just reading but also particular ways of talking about and using book language in their talk, is exemplified in studies carried out in this country. For example, Fox (1983) in a study of oral narratives showed how young children learn from books ways of keeping the audience interested and in suspense. Jack, aged six, ended one of his oral story tellings as follows: 'downstairs there was a noise. It is a noise that they have heard before – it's – it's of the big bad wolf carefully stepping in.' Like many of Jack's stories, this oral text could be traced to a story he had had read to him. In this case, Janet and Allan Ahlberg's *Burglar Bill* (1977) seems a major influence: 'Downstairs there is a noise. It is a noise that Burglar Bill has heard before; the noise of someone opening a window and climbing carefully in' (Fox, 1983, p. 21).

At first, Maintown seems to have much in common with Heath's second community Roadville, a white working-class community steeped for four generations in the textile mills.

Here, the children's nursery is full of nursery rhyme pictures, toys and mobiles and the child is encouraged to talk and given many opportunities to read. The difference highlighted by Heath in the literacy events is the way that parents use reading times as opportunities to teach, to get it right. Thus the child's first books tend to show single objects to be named. Parents often use wheels, zips and the like to introduce children to shapes, colours, movements, textures and so on. Stories tend to be 'real life', either written with simple wording or retold by the adult in simple sentences. Emphasis is thus on treating books as sources of information, often decontextualized, with few occasions where the children are encouraged to move their understanding into other contexts.

Significantly, Roadville children come to know stories as things that are found in books and the stories are not related or brought into real life. Any fictionalized account of a real events is viewed as a lie. 'Thus children cannot decontextualise their knowledge or fictionalise events known to them and shift them about into other frames' (Heath, 1982a, quoted in Mercer, 1988, p. 31). As the child gets older, book-reading becomes less interactive; it is an occasion when the child learns or is entertained. As school age approaches, children are introduced to workbooks, providing exercises for reading and writing, such as tracing letters, answering questions about stories, finding hidden words and so on, all reinforcing the notion that language breaks into smaller bits connected up with rules. Talking and reading are more clearly separated in Roadville interactions. Thus, directions to games are read but not talked about or even strictly followed, while daily tasks, like cooking, will be talked about but are not usually accompanied by reference to books such as manuals or recipes.

The third community looked at by Heath was Trackton which provides a further contrasting set of language uses. Trackton is a black working-class community, historically connected with agriculture but more recently getting work in the textile mills. A Trackton child enters an adult life without all the baby paraphernalia of mobiles, friezes and pop-up books. The rich language experience comes not from books but from the adult talk and oral narratives. There is little reading

material designed for children beyond Sunday school hand-
outs and there are no bedtime stories. Adults do not simulate
reading and writing behaviours and when older siblings play
at 'school time', adults are amused but do not actively build
on such occasions.

But the lack of books does not imply a lack of literacy. All
parents can read and engage in literacy events and by the
time a child enters school they can recognize and often read
printed information important in their lives such as signs,
labels, car names and even instructions. The literacy events
they will have watched and joined in before school include
negotiation over how to put a toy together, what a gas bill
notice means or how to fill in a voter registration form. The
Trackton reading behaviour seems far removed from the
descriptions found in curriculum guidelines. Reading is a
highly social activity in Trackton. Solitary reading without
oral explanation is viewed as strange, unacceptable and
indicative of a particular kind of failure which keeps an individual from being social. Meanings are negotiated by the
participants in the reading activities and thus the written
word is reshaped and reworked into an oral mode. Trackton
children 'live in an ongoing multiple-channeled stream of
stimuli, from which they select, practice, and determine the
rules of speaking and interacting with written materials'
(Heath, 1982b, p. 96). In contrast with Roadville, language
in Trackton is not decontextualized; real events are heavily
fictionalized and demand audience involvement. Print in isolation bears little authority.

The types of contrasts drawn among the different communities reflect the range of interactions possible under a label
such as 'reading a book'. Each group intertwines talk and
writing in very different ways. Such evidence questions any
binary oral-literate contrast, suggesting rather a set of features
that cross-classifies the groups. For example, Maintown and
Trackton value imagination and fictionalization, while Roadville does not. Direct teaching about language is valued in
Maintown and Roadville but not in Trackton. Negotiation over
the meaning of a book or letter is accepted practice in Trackton
and to some extent Maintown but not valued in Roadville.

Children are seen as needing their own specially designed reading materials in Maintown and Roadville but not in Trackton. When children, with their different experiences of interacting with print, enter school they will find that only some of their literacy practices are valued, and for some children the school literacy may seem very different from that found in their homes.

The contrasts among the three US communities described by Heath throw up important points. First, they highlight the range of language behaviours possible within one apparently circumscribed activity, a range which not only varies among social groups but also among age groups. Secondly, they serve as a salutary reminder that the experiences that children bring to school may be substantially different from those they will experience at school. There may even be direct conflict between the patterns of school and those of the community.

Another ethnographic study, this time of Athabascans in Alaska (Scollon and Scollon, 1981), further illustrates the culture-specific nature of literacy. The Scollons argue that different ways of using language reflect different cognitive orientations towards the world. Their work focuses on the inter-ethnic communicative difficulties that may arise when language practices differ in terms of the values, attitudes and ways of knowing. They argue that language patterns reflect a person's identity and to acquire a new form of literacy will have significant personal consequences. A few examples of differences in language use between Athabascans and mainstream Western schoolchildren will provide evidence for their argument.

Athabascans who consider themselves learners in a given context, e.g. children, are expected to observe and not to display their abilities to someone in a superior position, e.g. teachers and parents. This pattern of using language conflicts with the Western school tradition in which children are expected to show off what they know to the adult. Athabascans will also avoid conversations where the relationship between the participants is unknown and where the participants' views are unfamiliar. This is in contrast with the habit of English speakers to use language interactions to establish relationships and to learn about other people's opinions. One possible consequence of these differences is that typical school writing tasks where the audience is often unknown or fictionalized may present difficulties for the Athabascan. For Athabascans, the set of premises underlying the type of language that is highly valued in school – essays in which knowledge is displayed, the writer is placed in a dominant position, and the relationship with the reader is undefined – runs directly counter to the community's discourse patterns:

As a result, the acquisition of [Western school] literacy is not simply a matter of learning a new technology, it involves complicity with values, social practices, and ways of knowing that conflict with those of the Athabascans. (Gee, 1986)

Interactions in the classroom

The studies looked at here demonstrate how language learning is mediated through complex interactive and interpretive processes. We have each learned a set of language behaviours which we can draw upon when we talk, read and write. When knowledge is being communicated in schools, the individual interactive patterns of teacher and child may support or hinder the learning in different ways. An example of classroom interaction, taken from studies by Michaels (1981), may help to bring together some of the arguments.

Michaels collected samples of talk during 'sharing time' in an Infants' class and looked for differences in the children's use of discourse styles. 'Sharing time' in the American school studied is characterized by the children being asked if they have anything to share with the rest of the class. The sharing is a highly structured social event, with strict rules against other children interrupting the child who is talking. But it is also collaborative with the teacher and child building up the discourse together. What Michaels found was that the types of support given by the teacher reflected an underlying model of how the 'sharing' discourse should be organized. It should be on one topic, have a single speaker and form a coherent whole. It should make meanings explicit, i.e. not assume that meanings could be carried by intonation or gestures, and shifts in topic should be lexicalized. In other words, the teacher's implicit model of appropriate discourse shared many of the characteristics of expository writing (see chapter 2). For some children, this expected 'topic-centred' talk seemed easy to adopt and there could develop collaborative exchanges with the teacher. In Michaels' terms, there was synchrony between teacher and child. But other children, characteristically the black children in the class, used a 'topic-associating' style which did not match the teacher's model and which the teacher could not support through questions. Two extracts will illustrate the point:

Extract A: Topic-centred

(The original transcripts mark all the hesitations and intonation patterns in detail. Here, the transcription is simplified, marking only intonation groups and some pauses.)

MINDY: When I was in day camp/we made these/um candles
TEACHER: You made them?/
MINDY: And um/ I-I tried it with different colours/and with both of them but/one just came out/this one just came out blue/and I don't know/what this colour is/
TEACHER: That's neat–o/Tell the kids how you do it from the very start/Pretend we don't know a thing about candles/. . . OK/What did you do first?/What did you use?/Flour?/
MINDY: Um . . . there's some/hot wax/some real hot wax/that you/ just take a string/and tie a knot in it/and dip the string in the um wax/
TEACHER: What makes it uh have a shape?/
MINDY: Um/you just shape it/
TEACHER: Oh you shaped it with your hand/mm/
MINDY: But you have/first you have to stick it into the wax/then the water/and then keep doing that until it gets to the right size you want it/
TEACHER: OK/Who knows what the string is for?/

Extract B: Topic-associating

TEACHER: Deena/I want you to share some – one thing/that's very important/one thing/from where you are/ . . . is that where you are/is that where you were?/

DEENA: No/

TEACHER: OK/

DEENA: um/ . . . in the summer/ . . . I mean/ . . . w-when um/I go back to school/I came back to school/in September/ . . . I'm a have a new coat/and I already got it/ . . . and/ . . . it's/ . . . um/ . . . got a lot of brown in it/ . . . and/ . . . when/um/and I got it yesterday/ . . . and when . . . I saw it/my mum . . . my mother was going some . . . where/when my . . . when I saw it/ . . . on the couch/ and I showed my sister/and I was reading something out on . . . on the bag/and my big sister said/ (Aside: um close the door) my big sister said/Deena you have to keep that away/ from Keisha/'cause that's my baby sister/and I said no/ . . . and I said the plastic bag/ . . . because/ . . . um/ . . . when/ . . . um/ . . . sh-when the um . . . she was um (with me)/wait a minute/ . . . my/cousin and her/

TEACHER: Wait a minute/you stick with your coat now/I s-said you could tell one thing/ . . . that's fair/

DEENA: This was about my c–

TEACHER: OK all right/go on

DEENA: This was – and today/and yesterday when I . . . got my coat/my cousin ran outside/and he . . . ran tried to get him/and he/he he start/ . . . and when he get in my house/ . . . he layed on the floor/and I told him to get up because he was crying/

TEACHER: mm – what's that have to do with your coat?/

DEENA: h-he . . . becau– he wanted to go outside/but we . . . couldn't/ (exasperated)

TEACHER: Why?/

DEENA: 'cause my mother s-wanted us to stay in the house/

TEACHER: What does that have to do with your coat?/

DEENA: bec– um oh (whispers)

DEENA: because/. . . I don't know/

TEACHER: OK/thank you very much Deena/ (talking)

TEACHER: OK/do you understand what I was trying to do/Deena/I
           was trying to get her to stick with one/. . . thing/and
           she was talking about her/
CHILDREN: coat
TEACHER: new
CHILDREN: coat
TEACHER: coat/it sounds nice Deena/ (Michaels, 1981, pp. 431–2,
           435–6)

It is not clear that the stress placed by the teacher on 'one topic' is understood by Deena. She does have one topic: her coat and her cousin who, Michaels found out later, had tried to put his dirty hands on her new coat. She also has cohesion, albeit of a different sort expected by the teacher, linking her recollections by association and by intonation. But what Deena does not have is the required prose-like discourse style. Deena's, and others', different interpretation of the task may have significant effects on their acquisition of literacy.

More examples could be given (and the discussion of literacy in schools is a recurring theme throughout this book), but enough has been said, I hope, to make the point that there is no one 'autonomous' model of literacy (Street, 1984). Rather, one needs to see literacy as a set of social practices that are shaped by political and ideological factors so that some are more highly valued than others.

To return to the beliefs of schoolchildren interviewed about the value of writing, what the evidence suggests is that it is not simply a matter of learning to write that will lead to good jobs or to success in 'big school'. The extent to which literacy is an advantage depends on complex social factors, such as ethnicity, class and gender.

2

Writing and Speech

When we look at language *events* rather than language *systems* it is clear that writing practices are intertwined with talk and reading. The different modes of language are not separable in practice as they are in theory. However, the view that has prevailed for many years is one that describes writing in terms of its differences from speech. The dominance of this 'oral–literate tradition' is reflected in current curriculum models. For example, the National Curriculum for English (DES, 1989) clearly separates 'Writing' from 'Talk' and from 'Reading' in its Profile Components with little reference to their inter-relationships. Of course, it is convenient for analysts of language structure to isolate certain aspects of language for close inspection, but the separations made in theory can develop a false sense of reality so that we forget how much our use of one mode depends on our use of the other modes. Many current models of the writing curriculum are based on theories developed by linguists whose focus is on writing as a system. In order to evaluate current writing practices in schools, it is important to look at the particular contrasts that have been made between speech and writing.

The linguist's view of speech and writing

It is only quite recently that linguists have focused on the writing system as a separate area of study, distinct from speech. The beginnings of modern linguistics as the scientific study of language was marked by the identification of speech as the only proper object of attention. De Saussure, generally acknowledged as the founder of linguistics, argued that

Language and writing are two distinct systems of signs; the second exists for the sole purpose of representing the first. The linguistic object is not both the written and the spoken forms of words; the spoken forms alone constitute the object. (de Saussure, 1959 edn, pp. 23–4)

This was echoed by Bloomfield, who led the thinking of American linguistics, in his statement that 'Writing is not language, but merely a way of recording language by means of visible marks' (1935, p. 21).

Their argument for this view of the primacy of speech was based on historical and biological evidence. These include the fact that speech evolved before writing. The earliest written languages are dated around 3500 BC but speech probably dates from the beginnings of the human race, say a million years ago. As Stubbs (1980) puts it, the human race can be defined at *Homo loquens* as much as *Homo sapiens*. *Homo scribens*, however, was a much later attribution. While some societies still have not developed a written language, all have complex oral forms and, within any society with a written culture, speaking is the most frequent activity for virtually all individuals. Even children's claims that all they do in school is write is unlikely to be supported by a count of the number of words spoken and words written. The only exceptions to this talk–writing equation that come to mind are deaf-mutes or those who have taken a vow of silence. As further support for the primacy of speech, there is the argument that most (though not all) written forms of language attempt to represent the spoken language forms in some direct way through alphabets or syllabaries.

Biologically, the evidence is strong that we are designed to produce spoken language. Our vocal tracts have become specialized for the purpose of speaking, a development peculiar to humans as evidenced by the failure of attempts to teach animals to talk. And there seems to be an innate desire for all humans to talk, as shown by children's development of language under nearly all conditions – even deaf children engage in 'babbling' in their infancy. Writing does not seem to have as many biological determinants.

The arguments then for the primacy of speech are convincing. What is not convincing is the corollary that written language is purely derivative of speech. An equally valid argument seems to be that while speech came first, writing, when it did develop, came to have its own specialized functions, its own structural characteristics and its own importance.

A functional model of writing

A more profitable line of argument is a functional one, that takes as its starting point the view that language is a complex amalgam of functional variants. From this perspective, speech is not simply a system of sounds but represents many different ways of saying, of making meaning: differences that range from casual conversations to epic poems; or from a radio jingle to religious discourse. When written forms developed they added a new dimension to the variation, allowing new functions to develop, some closely related to speech forms, some quite distinct. For example, the very earliest written records suggest that writing first functioned for making lists and for administrative purposes with no direct spoken counterpart. In other words, writing did not come into existence simply as a new way of doing old things with language. As Halliday puts it:

[writing] came into being precisely so that *new* registers could be created: so that there could be a 'written language' that was not the same as the spoken . . . what emerges is a new range of functional variation. (1985, pp. 44–5)

Thus it is not enough to compare the two modes as linguistic systems; they have to be seen as functioning in different ways.

Making functional comparisons

A functional comparison of writing and speech allows one to look at the potential that each mode offers. Chafe (1982, 1985), for example, identifies two main dimensions that he feels distinguish the linguistic properties of speech and writing, differences that he argues emerge from the various processes involved. The first difference is the degree of *integration*. Writing tends to be more integrated and syntactically complex than speech; speech has a more fragmentary quality. This he attributes to the slower processing time needed for writing. Writing is considerably slower than speaking and more amenable to planning and editing. Furthermore, the readers of writing can process information more quickly than listeners. This makes it more acceptable in writing to have information-packed texts, i.e. the reader seems able to cope with a higher semantic load than the listener.

Chafe's second dimension is that of *interaction* which, he considers, ranges from the detached quality of writing to the involved quality of speaking. The act of writing tends to be a lone one, without necessary contact with the receiver. It therefore tends to be more detached, in contrast with spoken messages which are more usually conducted face-to-face and thus require high involvement between speaker and listener. This dimension is considered to be a very important one for understanding children's early writing, as young children will have little or no experience of using language without the receiver of the message being present (see chapter 6).

Other dimensions along which speech and writing can be placed have been suggested. For example, Tannen (1985) argues that speech tends to be socially-orientated while writing tends to be message-orientated, a difference that relates to the contexts in which the two modes are best suited, i.e. speech seems most appropriate for casual conversations while writing seems best suited for legal documents. A number of linguistic devices can be identified that show how writing manifests itself as more integrated and detached and how speech appears more fragmented and involved.

Achieving integration

Grammatical devices, typical of writing, which increase the integration and information load of language are those that decrease redundancy (e.g. by not repeating or rephrasing information) and increase the lexical density (e.g. by using various subordinating devices such as those described below). In speech, on the other hand, devices tend to be used that will increase redundancy and reduce lexical density. These include devices such as repetition, coordination and various ways of rephrasing. The following examples of integrating devices come from a popular supermarket 'check-out' magazine which clearly aims at a chatty style.

Use of nominals

In writing, a whole clause often becomes the noun phrase of another sentence in writing, where, in speech, two clauses would be used. Thus in writing we might find: 'The form that children's quarrels take largely depends on their age.' In speech, a less-integrated style might be: 'Children's quarrels are all different . . . and it largely depends on their age.'

Attributive adjectives

A noun phrase becomes more dense if the head noun is heavily modified *before* the main verb. This kind of density tends to be found in writing more often than in speech. Thus a written form might have the modified head noun as in: 'Big, chunky, interlocking shapes, just the right size for small hands to grasp, fit together in a number of different ways.' A spoken form, on the other hand, would be more likely to put adjectives in predicate position (and probably make other changes, such as using contractions): 'The shapes are big and chunky and they're interlocking. They're just right for little hands.'

Subordinate clauses

The use of subordinates is probably the most common way in which writing can be sculptured 'into complex products of more deliberate, leisurely creation' (Chafe, 1985, p. 111). Typically, dependent clauses are introduced by subordinators such as: 'if, although because, unless, when, whereas' and so on. In writing, subordinated constructions are commonly like: 'When it came to the question of what remedy brought the most relief to a sick child, a cuddle topped the list.'

Use of participles

Subordination is also commonly achieved in writing through the use of participles: 'Treated in this way, children will soon be up and running again.' This device is more commonly avoided in speech, unless you deliberately want to sound authoritative.

Other devices could be listed (see Perera, 1984; Chafe, 1985). What they all reflect is that writers can exploit clause structure in ways that will pack in a considerable amount of information, particularly around the noun phrase. The cost of using all its potential is that it can become hard to unpack. Here readers are at an advantage as they can reread the passage, though readers with all the time in the world may be defeated by some written structures, as anyone struggling over bureaucratic forms will know.

Achieving interaction

Chafe's second dimension was that of interaction, with writing being illustrated as more detached and speech as more involved. These different ends of a continuum result, in

Chafe's argument, from the fact that speech tends to be produced face-to-face, with more opportunities to involve the listener, while writing is often produced without the presence of the reader thus allowing the writer to be detached from the audience. The speaker is more concerned with the dynamics of the interaction, and needs to keep the listener involved if the communication is to continue. The writer, meanwhile, may be less concerned about the behaviour of the reader and less worried if the reader stops reading. Examples of language structures used in speech to show involvement include:

1   Use of phrases such as 'I mean . . . In my view . . . My feeling is . . .', which express the personal commitment of the speaker.
2   Use of phrases such as 'If you know what I mean . . . do you follow me?', which try to engage the listener's participation.
3   Use of direct quotations and the use of intensifiers such as 'really terrible', 'simply awful' to show the speaker's commitment to the subject.

Correspondingly, the detached writer is portrayed through such devices as the use of passives and the use of the impersonal pronoun 'one' instead of 'I'. These devices serve to distance the writer from the reader.

This dimension of integration maps onto a major difference often pointed out about the spoken and written modes. In speech, meanings can be conveyed through prosody and paralinguistic features, while in writing meanings and attitudes have to be expressed through words, with some support from punctuation strategies. Put another way, you cannot speak without also showing how you feel about what you are saying. But when you are writing, your facial expressions, hand gestures and audible sighs will not show up on the paper. Speech has qualities such as rhythm, intonation, loudness, pitch and pausing that have no counterparts in writing. These qualities lead, it is argued, to the dynamic nature of spoken interaction compared with the more impersonal style of writing.

Using different resources

The analysis of writing and speech presented by Chafe (and others) has a strangely competitive feel to it. One mode is made to sound inherently better than the other; or the two modes are described in terms of what they are missing: speech misses nominals; writing misses prosody. Often it seems that the strengths and weaknesses of each mode are overstated. So, for instance, while it is true that written products do not vary in loudness or pitch (leaving aside stage directions), this is not to say that writing cannot convey attitudes or show involvement with the reader. Of course it can, as any reading of letters received each morning will demonstrate. Writing has different resources available to it for conveying attitudes, in particular punctuation, where italics, capitals, brackets, exclamation marks, dashes and so on can and are used to a great extent for conveying meaning. Writing also has support from phrases such as 'don't take this to heart' or 'I mean this sincerely' which convey the writer's attitudes. The amount of meaning that can be conveyed in writing through punctuation and directions to the readers is particularly evident in young children's books where extensive use is made of different type fonts and of descriptions of how people are feeling. Anyone who has read aloud to a child will know how many paralinguistic features are available to the writer and, most importantly, how much children understand about these devices.

Written language has rhythm too, a property exemplified in its extreme form through poetry, but also present in the balancing of syntactic constructions achieved by the writers most pleasant to read. The power of writing to convey feelings is clearly evident in the many posters and advertisements where written language is used to great effect in the manipulation of feelings and attitudes.

While it is clearly unfair to see writing as the 'deprived' form when we are discussing the best modes for expressing attitudes, equally unfair is the representation of speech as the

unstructured 'form'. Descriptions like 'fragmentary', syntactically simpler, more redundant or lexically less dense all suggest
that speech is in some sense less sophisticated or even an
inferior form. This, as Halliday (1985) argues, comes about
partly because we too often compare finished written forms
with spontaneous speech. The written form has been edited
so that the planning processes are removed, while extracts of
conversations have all their hesitations left in. Furthermore,
speech and writing are usually compared in the printed form,
which gives an unfair advantage to writing. If certain written
texts were read aloud as though they were conversations there
would undoubtedly be as many criticisms of unintelligibility
as there is of speech written down. But when speech is analysed in its own terms, while it may be less lexically dense
and use fewer subordinating devices, it is by no means less
structured or less highly organized, it is just complex in a
different way.

Halliday talks about spoken language as being dynamic and
intricate. This he illustrates by showing how speakers relate
one clause to another, not as in writing through embedding
processes (e.g. subordination), but through complex sets of
dependencies where one clause expands, qualifies, restates or
exemplifies others, not only building on the speaker's own
utterances but also including the other speaker's contribution.
Because in conversations each speaker's turn is often quite
short, it may look in a transcript to be fragmentary, but if a
whole dialogue is studied a complex syntactic and semantic
web can be seen to be constructed between the speakers.
Halliday's argument goes further than demonstrating the different, but equally complex, forms of speech and writing. He
concludes that speech and writing impose different grids upon
experience: writing facilitating our understanding of the world
as things, speech creating a world of happenings.

Variants of the same system?

Distinctions can be made between speech and writing but
these emerge most clearly only when comparisons are made

between two particular variants of each mode: the spontaneous conversation and the essay-type or expository writing. It is these two types that are usually collected, analysed and contrasted (and the comparisons are usually made after speech has been converted into writing thus handicapping talk from the start). Apart from the actual differences in the channel of communication (and these days these are not just voice and paper but television, tape recordings, electronic mail, Fax, which all blur the edges between the original differences), the other differences seem best thought of as poles of a continuum. Bringing together some of the dimensions highlighted by Chafe and adding a few more from other researchers (Hudson, 1983), the following dimensions might be identified. Examples of writing and speech associated with different ends of each dimension are suggested.

Integration	*Fragmentation*
school textbook	shopping list
prepared lecture	informal chat
Detachment	*Involvement*
telephone directory	love messages
radio serial	telephone conversations
Message-orientated	*Socially-orientated*
recipe	birthday card
football commentary	'How do you do'
Context independent	*Context dependent*
story	car manual
poetry recital	oral directions

Other dimensions could be added such as 'use of Standard English', 'length', 'opportunities for revision' or 'visibility of receiver'. But the main message is that it is not enough to talk about writing and speech differences without saying first what speech activities and what writing activities are being compared.

Why is it that so much time is spent talking about differences in speech and writing – here and elsewhere – and making very clear distinctions between them in curriculum plans? The answer seems to be that speech and writing have developed in different culturally defined ways so that each has become more or less associated with particular social practices (e.g. writing for the expository account; speech for the expression of emotion). As Gee puts it:

What seems to be involved are different cultural practices that in certain contexts call for certain uses of language, language patterned in certain ways and trading on features like fragmentation and involvement to varying degrees. (Gee, 1986)

If it is the case that there is not so much one set of characteristics for speech and one set for writing, but rather that there are culturally defined ways of using speech and writing for different ends, then this throws up important questions. What are the alternative ways of patterning language in the two modes? Have linguists been focusing on far too narrow a range of written and spoken practices? With regard to the curriculum, in the name of providing access to success through literacy, have we been socializing children into mainstream ways of using language, ways that may be in conflict with children's own cultural practices with reading and writing? Should the 'writing lesson' provide far greater opportunities for children to explore the many variants of language – to look at what language can do rather than what it has become?

The issues raised by these questions, and a few possible answers, are directly addressed in later chapters. But before discussing writing practices in schools, some more background is needed about the nature of the writing task facing the child and the ways in which children tackle the learning task.

3

Symbols and Spellings

Children learning to write are surrounded by a mass of information about the way their society represents language in
writing – its orthography. A walk along any high street will
demonstrate the diversity of writing symbols from which children will begin to construct their view of literacy. For example,
there are street names, messages on posters and signs on shop
windows, most of which use alphabetic writing. But just as
prevalent are logographic symbols, such as 'P' for parking and
'M' for Macdonalds. There are pictograms such as road signs

Falling or
fallen rocks   Quayside or
river bank

and assorted symbols for ladies' and gents' lavatories. In
addition to these ways of representing language, there are
symbols which represent syllables, for example: '5 @ 50p'.
If we also include in a child's orthographic experiences the
examples of non-English scripts such as the Chinese or Arabic
writing displayed on restaurants and banks, then it is clear
that what children observe about their community's writing
system involves much more than the letters of the alphabet.

An incident with my own child brought home to me how
much children are taking in about the writing system and
how easy it is for an adult to develop 'tunnel vision' about
the principles of English orthography. On my daughter's third
birthday, she was given a sweatshirt on which was printed

It's fun being
3

I read this to her as 'It's fun being three'. Later, I overheard her saying to a friend: 'It says "it's fun being three bears".' And it does say that. I just hadn't seen the pictures as words.

When children begin to write, they may not have the experience to know which symbols to put in and which bits to exclude. As Temple et al. put it:

Discovering how to write in English involves making choices from a very large range of alternatives. Children may very well be more aware of the alternatives than adults are, because our long experience with alphabetic writing tends to blind us to the possibility that there may be ways of representing words with symbols that are different from the ways we do it. (Temple et al., 1982, p. 15)

To understand the nature of the task that children face, it is useful to think beyond our predominantly alphabetic writing system and to see how writing systems are organized and how they have developed. The writing systems available today have evolved over the past four or five thousand years and, not surprisingly, principles used in earlier systems remain alongside later ones. When children begin working out the principles governing their own community's writing system, they often come up with solutions which apply in systems other than their own.

Three main ways of coding language in writing are in current use:

1 Alphabetic writing where symbols represent units of sound (phonemes).
2 Syllabic writing where symbols represent syllabic units of sound.
3 Logographic writing where symbols represent linguistic units of meaning (morphemes).

A brief history of writing

Although we cannot be exactly sure how the earliest writing systems came about, it is reasonably clear that their origins lie in pictures. At some point in human development, pictures used for representing objects and events began to be used as symbols which could be combined to communicate messages. At first, such messages used symbols to represent ideas. This meant that the writer's message could be worked out, but it could be interpreted by the reader in a number of ways. Downing and Leong (1982) quote an example of idea-writing from a North American Indian tribe, the Ojibwa (figure 3.1). The X at the centre stands for the gesture of crossed arms, meaning a deal or exchange. The message expressed the idea that skins of buffalo, weasel and otter are offered for a rifle and 30 beaver skins (Downing and Leong, 1982, p. 53).

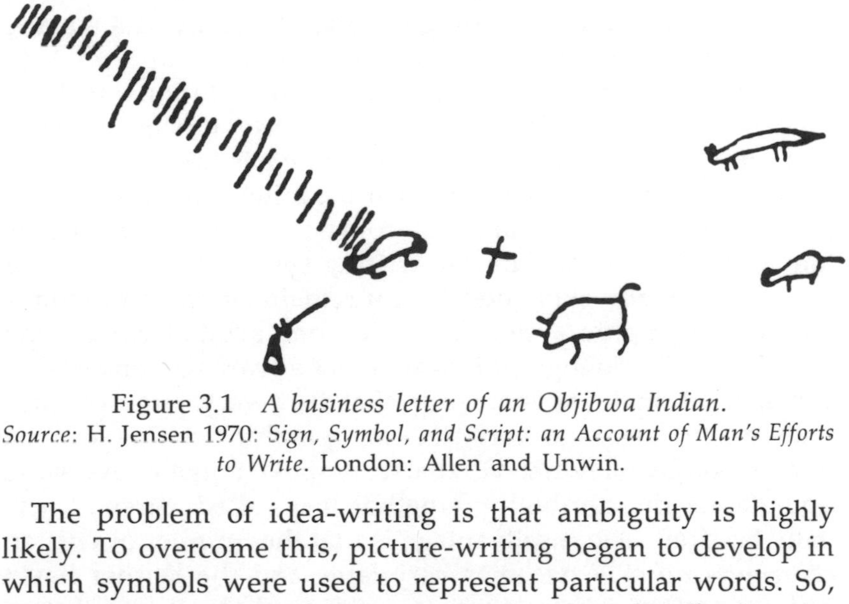

Figure 3.1   *A business letter of an Objibwa Indian.*
Source: H. Jensen 1970: *Sign, Symbol, and Script: an Account of Man's Efforts to Write*. London: Allen and Unwin.

The problem of idea-writing is that ambiguity is highly likely. To overcome this, picture-writing began to develop in which symbols were used to represent particular words. So, for example, in China, some time in the second millenium BC, the picture for 'horse' which had represented the class of animals now stood for the word 'horse' (figure 3.2). It could thus be read aloud and it could only be read in one way: from being a picture for an idea it had become a character for a word. For most researchers it is only at this point that the system of communication is technically classed as writing: when what is encoded by the writer is decoded by the reader in exactly the intended ways.

Figure 3.2   *The earliest known form of Chinese character 'horse'.*
Source: M. A. K. Halliday 1985: *Spoken and Written Language*. Victoria: Deakin University Press, p. 15.

The word-pictures, or pictograms, became more and more stylized. Their form usually varied according to the writing tools and material used which included incising on bone, chiselling on clay and painting on silk. Gradually, the writing system was extended to include symbols for words that do not have any immediate pictorial representation, such as 'understand', 'today' or 'of'. (More accurately, it is morphemes that are symbolized, not words. Morphemes are the smallest grammatical units that distinguish meaning. Thus, for example, the single work 'unpack' consists of two morphemes 'un' + 'pack'.) In the Chinese writing system, the number of characters greatly expanded, and it remains today a predominantly logographic system in which one symbol equals one morpheme. The logographic system has advantages and disadvantages. A main advantage is that in a very large country with many language varieties, logographic writing can be understood by all, whatever dialect is spoken, just as everyone undertands the symbol '3' whether it is called 'three', 'tres', 'tatu' or 'drei'. The disadvantage is that the number of written characters quickly becomes very large and the learner has a difficult task of memorizing so many symbols. It is a system that seems to have more advantages for the reader than for the writer.

In the independently developed Sumerian cuneiform system and the Egyptian hieroglyphic system, writers took one key principle a step further than the Chinese. This was the rebus principle whereby a symbol that was used for one word could also be used for another word with the same sound. Thus, an arrow was used in Sumerian for the word 'ti' ('arrow'), but an arrow was also used for 'ti' meaning 'life'. In this system longer words can be made up of symbols used for mono-syllables so you only need as many symbols as there are monosyllabic words in the language. (The underlying prin-ciple is the same as that used in charades where words like 'bombadier' are acted out as 'bomb', 'bad' and 'ear'.) An easy step from this is to make each symbol represent a syllable. Thus instead of a 'charactery' there develops a syllabary. The script, once fully syllabic, becomes a phonological one in which each symbol represents a consonant and vowel sound. A syllabary is best suited to languages whose words generally have two or three consonants separated by vowels, that is, have few consonant clusters. Ancient Phoenician and modern Japanese are examples. In Japanese, there are 46 different syllables in the Kana syllabary and with these every word of Japanese can be constructed. In addition, Japanese use Kanji, which are logographic characters, but young children learn to read and write using only Kana symbols.

English orthography is predominantly alphabetic and evolved from the Ancient Greek system. The Greeks took over the Phoenician syllabary. However, given the nature of Greek with strings of consonants before a vowel, a syllabic system was inappropriate. They therefore adopted the Phoenician symbols, and added a few new ones, but used them to rep-resent each consonant and vowel sound separately. Thus the alphabet was formed (named after the first two syllables 'aleph' and 'beth' in the Phoenician system) in which each symbol represents a sound or, more accurately, a phoneme, i.e. a unit of sound that can distinguish word meaning.

From the Greek system, the two main European alphabets are derived. The present day Russian writing system developed from the Cyrillic system which came directly from the Greek one, with a few new letters. The Latin alphabet, on which English is based, was developed by the Romans from the Etruscan system which was itself derived from the Greek. The Roman alphabet arrived in Britain in the sixth century when the Anglo-Saxons were converted to Christianity. It was supplemented by runic symbols for phonemes not represented in Latin. One example is þ called 'thorn' to represent 'th' sounds. This was later represented by printers as 'Y', a form that survives in 'Ye Olde Teashoppe'.

This brief history of orthography may give the impression that writing systems are easily classified as logographic, syllabic or alphabetic. This is far from being the case. Given their long historical evolution and the history of borrowing from each other, each orthography is a mixture of systems. Many logographic characters are used in English. A quick look at my keyboard produces: 1 2 3 4 5 6 7 8 9 0 £ $ % & * # + and =. English can also be exploited as a syllabic and logographic system, as in 'Bar-B-Q', 'R U 18?' and 'I♡NY'.

English is, of course, far from strictly alphabetic, with a less than one-to-one correspondence between sound and symbol; a fact that has led to many suggestions of spelling reform. For many, the English spelling system is a mess in need of radical overhaul. For others, the messiness is seen as a sensible compromise between competing ways of representing the complexities of speech. Before turning to accounts of how children do cope with its complexities, it is worth considering the English spelling system and how it represents sounds, on the grounds that understanding how our orthography works is more fruitful than criticizing its absurdities.

The importance of spelling

I was at a meeting of various language researchers recently that was looking at ways of assessing children's writing. We all agreed that children's ability to write in different ways for different purposes and in different social contexts was more important than their ability to spell. We wanted to find assessment techniques that would see spelling and punctuation as surface features: aspects that could be less than perfect without diminishing the central worth of a pupil's work. The discussion had a comfortable but rather nebulous feel to it, as we exchanged ideas about successful writing practices. After about an hour, someone raised the issue of spelling. At once the meeting became animated. Everyone had a view and positions were quickly taken by the participants. At last, there seemed to be something tangible to talk about and something that we felt confident to analyse when faced with a child's writing.

Most of us have similar anecdotes to tell of our double standard towards spelling. We claim that it is not too important; that it is the message that counts, and yet we pay disproportionate attention to our own and other people's spelling inadequacies. Given such adult behaviour and attitudes to spelling, in deed if not in spirit, it is hardly surprising that when children are asked what is most important about writing, the majority give answers that refer to spelling and handwriting. When asked what is difficult about writing, as many children give answers such as 'writing on the lines' and 'getting the spellings right' as they give answers about 'knowing what to say and how to say it' (see chapter 5).

Spelling is undeniably important. It can (though rarely does) make the difference between an intelligible and an unintelligible message. But more than being linguistically important, it is socially important. It is often used as the criterion for distinguishing the educated from the uneducated (albeit inaccurately as many highly educated people are poor spellers and vice versa). Spelling failure is frequently drawn upon as a means of monitoring the 'state of the nation' in media reports. It is these social attitudes that largely come into play when we correct children's writing, as young children's writing is rarely unintelligible because of its spelling. While the social attitudes cannot be ignored, they need to be recognized and put in perspective as they are not useful for the less-competent and less-confident writer. Children who learn early that spelling it right is the key to success may well be inhibited from getting their own message down. They may choose the safe words rather than the higher risk ones, or they may refuse to write at all when the odds on getting the spelling right seem so stacked against them.

An idiosyncratic invention?

As spelling plays such a central role in both writing and our lives, it is worth examining just how accurate our notions are about its organization. There is a prevailing myth that spelling is more full of exceptions than rules, that it is a disaster area full of historical accidents in urgent need of reform. While the system is certainly complex, closer inspection shows it to be far from arbitrary in its organization. Its complexity reflects not so much sadism on the part of its designers as the difficulty of accommodating the conflicting needs of its users. The spelling system needs to be helpful to the reader and thus tries to have as few ambiguities as possible – relatively few words that sound the same are spelled the same. At the same time, the system needs to be easy for the writer to learn with the letters representing the sounds as closely as possible. At once there is conflict between the reader's and the writer's needs. A second conflict arises from the desire to have a system that reflects the way people talk and yet, at the same time, to have one that does not favour one particular group of speakers. The desire to be relatively neutral in the representation of different accents conflicts with the motivation for a close letter:sound correspondence.

The commitment to an alphabetic system creates a third problem as it opposes a system in which words that are related grammatically and lexically look like each other. Thus it is useful for words like 'sign' and 'signature' to look alike even though that means that phonological principles have to be sacrificed. With so many contradictory principles in operation, it is no wonder that spelling reforms are constantly called for but never satisfactorily enacted. The main deterrent to change is the complexity of the current system which means that minor tinkering with one part of the system will have knock-on effects to other parts. Stubbs sums up the spelling system by saying that 'far from being optimal, the English spelling system represents, on the contrary, a fairly good compromise solution to several incompatible demands' (Stubbs, 1980, p. 66).

The current view of spelling organization is that it is multi-code in which spelling conventions can signal a number of different relationships. While English orthography primarily represents sounds, it has other overlapping codes. Some examples will help illustrate the coding system.

Grammatical codes

A striking example of grammatical spelling conventions is the use of 's' or 'es' to indicate plurals, possessives, contractions and the third person present tense as in: dogs; Jamie's books; Jason's going; Sara wish*es* to stay. The actual sound represented by the letters 's' or 'es' varies: it is /s/, /z/ or /iz/, as in the final sound of 'dogs', 'cats' and 'horses'. But the different sounds are not identified in the spelling as it is considered more important to reflect their grammatical relationship than it is to draw attention to their phonetic differences. Which sound is represented by the 's' letter is predictable by the reader able to draw on linguistic knowledge.

The pronunciation rule for the spelling 's' is: (a) after sibilant or affricate sounds (e.g. /s/, /f/, /tʃ/, /z/) the ending is /iz/; (b) after voiced sounds (e.g. /b/, /d/, /g/) the ending is /z/; (c) after unvoiced sounds (e.g. /p/, /t/, /l/) the ending is /s/. One advantage of this spelling code for grammatical markers is that it allows you to distinguish certain pairs of words whose pronunciation is the same but whose grammatical status is different. For example, in the pairs mince/mints; tax/tacks the second in the pair is spelled with a final 's' to mark its plural status.

A similar principle controls the spelling of the past tense 'ed' which, as a general rule, is written 'ed' even when its pronunciation is /t/ (e.g. in 'walked'), /d/ (e.g. in 'rained') or /id/ (e.g. in 'wanted'). Such a code helps the reader determine that 'bold' is not a verb but 'bowled' is. But it is generalities that are being talked about not immutable rules; 'sold', for instance, does not conform. Sometimes a coding principle can coexist with another one; sometimes it is in conflict.

Lexical codes

The spelling system also likes to show lexical relationships between words often at the cost of obscuring the pronunciation. For example, 'malign' might seem a strange way to spell the word whose pronunciation has no 'g' sound. But the presence of the 'g' reflects the lexical relationship between 'malign' and 'malignant'. Similar patterns are found in 'paradigm/paradigmatic', 'medical/medicine', 'grammar/grammatical', 'resign/resignation'. But there are exceptions here too, such as 'pronounce/pronunciation' and 'explain/explanation'.

The English spelling system also likes to show which words are unrelated in meaning despite similar sounds. It therefore reduces the potential number of homographs by using different spellings: e.g. 'write/right/rite'; 'doe/dough'. As with many of the other principles, such conventions seem to be designed to support the reader, but do little for the writer's confidence. There is also an interesting lexical code that reserves the use of two-letter words for grammatical words (e.g. to, in, so), while using three-letter words for lexical items (e.g. two, inn, sew). Exceptions here exist, notably in nicknames, e.g. Jo, Al and Di.

Cultural preference principles

Spelling is also affected by some cultural preferences for word shape. This is a rather unreliable set of principles determined by emotional or aesthetic reactions to spelling. One example is the retention of 'gh' at the beginning of a small set of words with similar negative overtones; ghoul; ghost; ghastly. At one time 'gh' was used for many other words including 'gherle' and 'ghoos', but most 'gh' beginnings were dropped except those which seemed to have slightly sinister connotations. (Though, as Stubbs, 1980, points out, through a historical accident, 'gherkins' and 'Ghurkas' ended up in rather poor company.)

Historical accidents

The history of spelling (see Scragg, 1974) is a tale of accidents and overzealous reforms, the legacies of which thwart many a speller. For example, Renaissance enthusiasm for classical roots to show in the language led to words such as 'science' gaining the 'sc' beginning in order to show its Latinate origins. But etymological zeal was not always matched with knowledge and so today we have 'scent' and 'scissors' whose 'sc' falsely reflects a Latin root. Many changes have depended on entrepreneurial activity without much central control resulting in some piecemeal change. So, for instance, when sound changes led to a contrast between the /tʃ/ sound as in 'chat' and the /k/ sound as in 'cat', sounds which had previously not distinguished meaning, scribes took from the French the letters 'ch' to represent /tʃ/. This new graphic symbol was quickly accepted throughout the system. On the other hand, a comparable pronunciation change that led to a distinction between the sounds ð and ϴ , as in 'then' and 'thin', was not followed by the introduction of a new symbol: 'th' has to serve both sounds. Little wonder that there are calls for a body like the Académie Française to oversee the development of the English spelling system.

Beyond spelling

To describe the orthographic system fully, important non-phonemic devices need to be mentioned – devices that are often taken for granted until the writing of young children is looked at. These include which way to write: left to write, right to left or up and down; when to leave a space; and how to help the reader capture the writer's meaning and attitudes. In speech, intonation and other paralinguistic features carry much of the meaning of the message. Writing, too, has its own comparable system.

An important convention in English is that writing goes from left to right, a characteristic not shared by all languages familiar to children in Britain. Interestingly, in their development of a writing system, the Greeks initially wrote from right to left. Then they tried writing right to left and left to right on alternate lines, so that the pen never leaves the paper. Finally, they adopted a left to right direction. When children are working out the directionality principle, they sometimes reach most logical, if incorrect, conclusions. For instance,

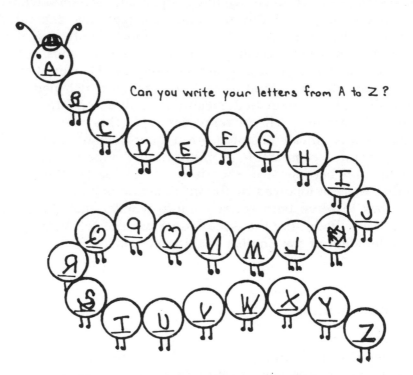

Can you write your letters from A to Z ?

Figure 3.3   *One child's solution to directionality.*
Source: C. A. Temple, R. G. Nathan and N. A. Burris 1982: *The Beginnings of Writing*. Boston: Allyn and Bacon, p. 39.

Temple et al. (1982) give an example of a child who was required to write the alphabet in a curling caterpillar (figure 3.3). A Cleveland child thought through the problem even further when he found that his account of 'Lemon Trees' spread over two pages (figure 3.4). Orientation is experimented with a lot in young children's early writing, often consciously. A nursery child in a Newcastle school pointed to her 'writing' at the top of her drawing saying 'That's my name. I've written it backwards for a change.'

Spaces between words are important signals to the reader that may not be obvious to the young writer – historically,

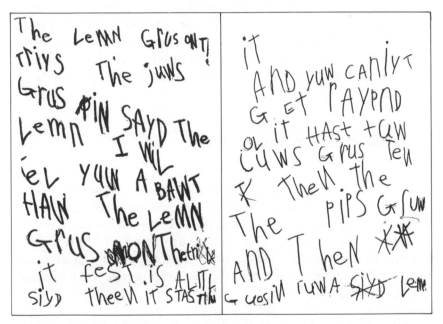

Figure 3.4 *Christopher's 'Lemon Trees'. Note: You need to read down the left-hand page and then up the right-hand one: an interesting solution to the problem of continuous texts. 'The lemon grows on the trees. The juice grows inside the lemon. I will tell you about how the lemon grows on the tree. It first is a little seed. Then it starts growing into a lemon and then the pips grow. Then the juice grows then all it has to do is to get ripened and you can eat it.'*
Source: National Writing Project 1989a: *Becoming a Writer*. Walton-on-Thames: Thomas Nelson, p. 85.

they were a fairly late development. There are no spaces as such between words in speech and to use a space in writing involves a child knowing where word boundaries are. For some words the beginnings and ends can be worked out fairly well, but there are those words whose edges are blurred such as 'alot', 'into' and 'alright'.

Punctuation is a further crucial orthographic device that children both see and experiment with in their early writing, for example, in a series of letters sent from nursery children to a fictional character 'Joe, the Ladybird' (figures 3.5a and b). There was no explicit teaching of punctuation in the nursery, but the child had observed question marks in other people's writing and had learned some of the principles of their use. Perhaps too often ignored are the non-phonemic devices such as italics, bold, underlining and many different type fonts. Any quick glance at current popular children's fiction, especially comics, shows how such devices are exploited.

From the child's point of view

The examples of letters to 'Joe the Ladybird' raise important issues about the development of orthography. Both Emily and Joel have been closely observing the way messages are written. In their nursery, they have been supported in their observations by the teacher's talk about writing and by their reading of all the print around them. Among the conventions being learned are:

Emily: left-to-right directionality; spaces between words; use of question mark; use of signature at the end of a message; some phonemic principles.

Joel: left-to-right directionality, though with some modifications to the rule when space runs out; speech bubbles; the use of Xs for kisses; use of name at the end of message; spelling of a number of words.

Figure 3.5 *Letters to Joe the Ladybird sent by (a) Emily and (b) Joel.*
Source: National Writing Project 1989c: *Audiences for Writing*; Walton-on-
Thames: Thomas Nelson, pp. 14 and 15.

While it is clear that the children are acquiring the adult orthographic rules, a close examination of these two children's writing shows that they are not simply imitating the adult orthographic system, they are hypothesizing about and experimenting with orthographic principles. For example, both Emily and Joel have used a syllabic-type principle in their representation of 'are' as 'R' and 'you' as 'U'. Perhaps all the information they receive about the alphabet has led them to assume that the letter name can also represent the one-syllable word: after all, if you can use the single letter 'I' for the first person, it is logical to assume you can use 'U' for the second person. Emily's use of 'Y' for 'you' may mark a sort of transitional stage when she has learned about the letters used in the adult world but still tries to use a syllabic approach.

When children are learning how to spell, they are learning to make sense of the adult system and creating their own system of rules based on pretty logical, if not always correct, assumptions. To understand how children cope with the complexities of the adult orthographic system it is important first to understand just how that system operates, how the codes and conventions coexist and conflict with each other. Secondly, we need to understand how children take in available information about the system and actively incorporate new principles into their writing. The pattern of development of writing for each individual child is a dynamic one, involving successive elaborations and refinements on his or her theories. An example from a Manchester child illustrates the way a child experiments with and constructs spelling (figure 3.6).

Young children's early attempts at spelling are often described as 'invented'. It is a term that gained popularity because it changed the focus from looking at children's errors – what the children have so far failed to learn about the adult system – to one which looked at children's experiments – how children are constructing the spelling system for themselves. The child-as-inventor is seen as active and creative, not so much making mistakes in spelling, but working out novel ways of coping with the complexity of the system. The attitude seems a healthy one and one that has a parallel in theories of learning to talk. When a two-year-old, for example, says 'I

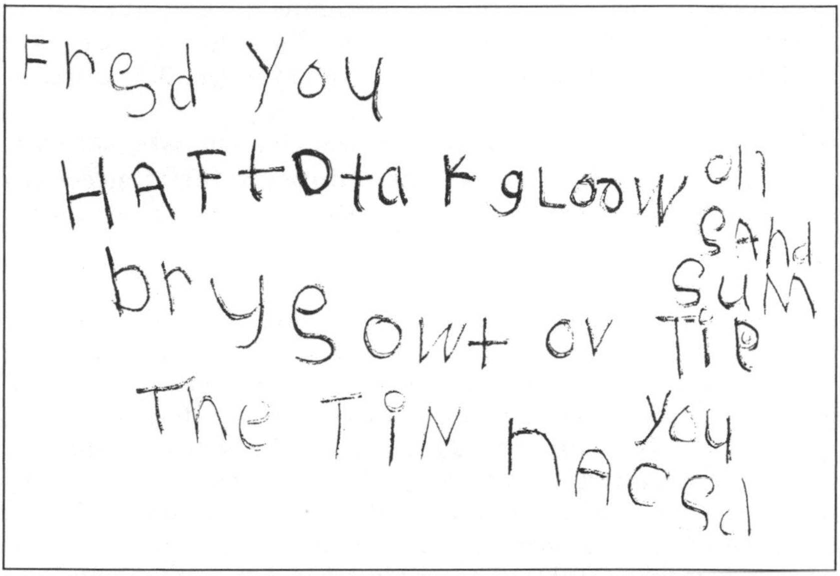

Fred you
HAFtOta k gLoow oll
brye owt ov sand sum
The Tin nace you

Figure 3.6   *Sandra: early experiments with spelling. 'First, you have to
take (the) glue brush out of the tin. Next you tip some sand on.'*
Source: National Writing Project 1989a: *Becoming a Writer*. Walton-on-
Thames: Thomas Nelson, p. 74.

runned and runned', we applaud the ability of the child to
generate the past tense '-ed' rule, rather than consider the
sentence as in need of immediate correction. Similarly, a child
who points to her father in the shower and says 'daddy
raining' is seen as using her limited language knowledge as
resourcefully and creatively as possible not as someone failing
to learn the system. When we look at children's writing, it
seems most productive to view 'errors' as reflecting points in
a child's development and as attempts to create meaning
despite the lack of knowledge of the whole system.

However, the word 'invented' needs a bit more interro-
gation as it can suggest that the child is some kind of sole
operator, working it all out for herself. The successful speller
may give the impression it all happened in a smooth unaided
fashion, with the system being gradually refined until the
spelling matched that of the adult. But this denies the importance of those around who direct attention to the features and

principles of the orthography. It also fails to suggest the type of support needed for those whose spelling does not develop well. Spelling, like all other aspects of language, is learned in interaction with others.

Margaret Peters (1985) discusses the characteristics of children who have 'caught' spelling through their successful engagement with the adult rules. She describes the process thus:

Spelling is not . . . 'caught' just through reading. It is certainly not through listening, since the English spelling system can have more than one spelling for any one sound, e.g. cup, done, does, blood, tough, and more than one sound for any one spelling, e.g. does, goes, canoe. It is almost certainly 'caught' in the early years through looking in a specially intent way. It is 'caught' through the child's developing forms of imagery and serial reconstructions and, as a consequence of this, becoming accustomed to the probability of letter sequences occurring. The children who have 'caught' spelling are familiar with these sequences in the world around them. They are . . . sensitised to the coding of English and this is in a benign social context where parents and teachers are reviewing, commenting on and predicting events in the child's day, e.g. shared activities which are regulated by the child in speech and writing. (Peters, 1985, p. 37)

The child's sensitivity to the coding of English has been demonstrated in many classrooms where emphasis is on facilitating children's construction of the system through talking about and illustrating the characteristics of written language. Stephen Cummings, a nursery teacher in London who participated in the National Writing Project, collected many examples of children's work to demonstrate this point. In his classroom much time was spent reading and talking about books, and the children's early writing reflected their growing awareness of writing conventions. One child, Hang, for example, produced at Halloween time an illustration clearly derived from Pienkowski's Meg and Owl characters but with her own text (figure 3.7). Another child, Juliana, showed her awareness of the interrelationship of text and illustration in her information about the dietary requirements of the frog (figure 3.8).

Figure 3.7 *Hang: Halloween picture with original text.*
Source: National Writing Project 1989a: *Becoming a Writer*. Walton-on-Thames: Thomas Nelson, p. 66.

Figure 3.8 *Juliana: text and illustration interrelated.*
Source: National Writing Project 1989a: *Becoming a Writer*. Walton-on-Thames: Thomas Nelson, p. 67.

Figure 3.9   *David: showing detailed knowledge of the use of writing.*
Source: National Writing Project 1989a: *Becoming a Writer*. Walton-on-
Thames: Thomas Nelson, p. 66.

Figure 3.10   *Juliana: 'Jack and the Beanstalk' with musical score.*
Source: National Writing Project 1990c: *A Rich Resource: Writing and Language
Diversity*. Walton-on-Thames: Thomas Nelson, p. 36.

Figure 3.11 *Nga: writing in both Chinese and English.*
Source: National Writing Project 1989a: *Becoming a Writer*. Walton-on-
Thames: Thomas Nelson, p. 34.

Many pieces of work collected showed the amount of detailed information that children of nursery age have about the use of writing. David's work includes his name on the car and a number on the church (figure 3.9).

Stephen Cummings was particularly interested in children's fascination with and sensitivity to the print around them and experimented one day by putting up on the nursery wall various examples of musical notation, without comment. Soon afterwards he found that the children's writing contained some musical notes alongside their letters. He then began talking about how to write music and was rewarded with texts such as this musical version of 'Jack and the Beanstalk' from Juliana (figure 3.10).

The provision in this nursery of a very rich print environment and the teacher's active encouragement of children to use their knowledge about language in their writing seems to be the way in which children can 'catch' spelling. It is a learning context that supports the children's experimentation and does not channel them down a narrow adult-conceived route to spelling mastery. In this particular nursery many of the children were bilingual and had knowledge of other written languages. Cummings found that when the print environment contained examples from their home languages, there was an extraordinary volume of bilingual writing occurring in the writing of both bilingual and monolingual children (figure 3.11). This suggests that the sensitizing process described by Peters (1985) does not simply consist of drawing attention to written language; it also involves adults showing the value they place on different sorts of writing, and encouraging children to see writing as far more than mastery of the English orthographic system.

4

Becoming a Writer

Children's discoveries about their world are fascinating to observe. As they work out how to stack beakers, use a spoon, throw objects off the table or climb a slide, we can speculate about the physical and mental abilities that are necessary for such achievements to take place. And when children as young as two and three are able to talk so competently, they challenge our explanations of learning. Can such learning be explained by some innate mechanism controlling development? How much learning depends on imitation of adults? Is there a fixed order of development? How do different environments affect the rate of development? Answers to such key questions implicitly or explicitly underlie classroom approaches to different aspects of learning. A classroom, for example, where young children spend considerable time copying letters beneath their teacher's clear handwriting and are expected to get every spelling correct in the first draft runs on assumptions about learning that are very different from those of a classroom where children choose what to write and where children's invented letter shapes and spellings are accepted and encouraged.

Studies of young children's language development have, since the late 1960s, emphasized the role of the child as language-maker, working out the rules of language, often very creatively, fine-tuning them and gradually moving towards the adult language system. The child has been seen as actively involved in working out the adult system, neither merely copying the adults around her, nor waiting for formal instruction before learning something new. But while this active role has been given to the young talker, a very different role has often been given to the young writer. Until quite recently the acquisition of written language was assumed to be a secondary form of learning, something that was learned once a child went to school, through formal instruction.

A prevalent assumption seems to have been that children have had little experience of writing or writers before they go to school and once instruction begins, writing can be introduced in a strictly ordered fashion: letter shapes first, then combinations of letters into words and finally written messages. Hall illustrates how unquestioned this assumption has been by quoting from a leaflet sent out by a Local Education Authority in 1983. It states:

Unlike talking, writing does not occur naturally to most people and before writing one has to learn how to. Young children learn to form writing patterns, then form letters and from them words and sentences. (Hall, 1987, p. 41)

What is so surprising is that no recognition is given to children's knowledge about what writing is and what it does before they come and are introduced to the adult orthographic system at school.

The view expressed by this LEA that letter-forming comes first, mechanics before meaning, is to be seen in most of the published preschool materials, activity books and the like, and in the popular magazines for parents. They all emphasize the preparation that is needed for writing in terms of pencil control, pattern-making, copying and shape recognition. For example, *Practical Parenting* (November 1989) had a four-page special on developing writing which included the following:

There are three different types of pre-writing activity you can practise with your child: general games to help him get used to different ways of using his hands, pencil games to help him control the pencil before you introduce 'real' writing, and writing games that introduce letters and words.

The games include cutting-out, pom-pom making, sewing,

tracing and so on. There is a clear, explicit message that there are things to do before 'real' writing can develop and, crucially, that it is the adult who introduces writing at the appropriate moment.

Early writing lessons

Given these assumptions about preschoolers' writing beha-viour, it is hardly surprising that few studies have been made of the writing children do 'naturally' before school. Those who have studied the young child's language environment have collected few examples of writing. Hall (1987) argues that children's early writing has often been missed or dismissed by parents as well as by researchers. While parents eagerly anticipate their child's first words, however far they are from the adult forms, many parents may not recognize early 'scrib-ble' as the precursor to later writing. If little value is given to early attempts to write then opportunities for practising writ-ing may be restricted to adult-controlled contexts, such as writing their names on greeting cards. However, when parents are encouraged to observe and 'read' their children's early writing, a new perspective on writing development emerges.

A nice example of this came from a Cleveland nursery where the teachers began observing young children's writing and discussing their observations with parents. They found that parents had often not seen the value of children's experiments with writing at home but soon became involved once they realized their role in the child's learning processes. One child, Christopher, for example, was observed writing with his friend in the nursery 'office'. He had several sheets of paper folded together as a book and, when he had completed three pages of text, he also found and folded a coloured sheet of paper. He carried his book around explaining that it was a newspaper with its colour supplement. When his mother collected him he was still carrying it and the teacher suggested that he take it home. His mother was pleased by the interest in this writing and the value placed on a four-year-old's newspaper. At home, the family became involved. Christopher's father asked him to find out what was on television, while his brother wanted to read the football page. And so the paper went to and from school for a week with the new articles being commented on each night (figure 4.1).

Teachers in the National Writing Project who began collecting samples of young children's work that were produced in the 'writing corner', in the 'café', 'post office' or by the 'telephone' were often surprised and fascinated by the amount of writing engaged in by children when opportunities were provided. Those opportunities that simulated adult writing contexts, such as taking telephone messages, taking orders or filling in forms stimulated a great range of different writing behaviours. The uses of writing were often highly resourceful.

For example, Alison, in a Newcastle nursery, demonstrated her understanding of the power of writing when she asked her teacher, Michelle Huart, if she could go to Soft Play. She was told that she was not on the list that week. Alison walked

Figure 4.1   *Christopher's 'newspaper'.*
Source: National Writing Project 1989a: *Becoming a Writer*. Walton-on-Thames: Thomas Nelson, p. 23.

away, reappearing several minutes later with a piece of paper saying, 'Miss Huart, I can go to Soft Play because I'm on the list. Look!' (figure 4.2). Faced with writing like this it becomes necessary to talk about writing development not simply in terms of the order in which to introduce the writing system, but in terms of the opportunities that need to be available for children to explore and construct adult writing behaviour.

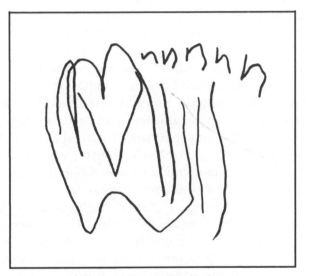

Figure 4.2   *Alison's 'list'.*
Source: National Writing Project 1989a: *Becoming a Writer*. Walton-on-Thames: Thomas Nelson, p. 13.

Models of writing development

A number of researchers have looked at young children's writing and tried to suggest developmental models to explain early forms. Clay (1975) looked closely at what children produced in their early writing experiments and suggests certain principles that children seem to follow, though not necessarily in a particular order. Among the principles that she uses to describe samples of early writing are: the *flexibility* principle

– children experimenting with graphic symbols, creating new ones and decorating known ones; the *inventory* principle – children taking stock of what they know about writing; the *generating* principle – children using a few known symbols and some rules for their combination to create new forms. Clay's descriptive categories build up a picture of a young child playing and experimenting with the writing system: repeating its patterns; trying out novel combinations; listing everything they can remember; seeing what it looks like backwards; imitating observed patterns and so on. They reflect behaviours that do not seem to occur in any fixed order but happen alongside each other. They are reminiscent of the language behaviours noted by researchers of oral language development. Such play-like behaviour in early writing can be illustrated with many examples. The writing samples below come from teachers and parents involved in the National Writing Project (NWP, 1989a) who began, at first informally, and later more systematically, to see what nursery children were writing outside any formal instruction.

Saiqa, from Manchester, produced a notebook in a classroom 'café' (figure 4.3). She appears to be imitating observed forms from Urdu/Arabic and English, demonstrating what she knows about the different orthographic systems (e.g. directionality) and repeating known forms. Naomi, a Cleveland nursery child, wrote a letter to her cousin using her limited set of letters and numbers in various sequences to create her message (figure 4.4). Christopher, also from Cleveland, combines a number of different writing strategies in his description (figure 4.5). He read the message as 'The Hulk is standing on a snake and Batman has got his pole.' Close study of the text shows considerable knowledge of alphabetic principles (e.g. BADMAN – Batman; POL – pole) and possibly some syllabic principles, where one letter represents a whole word or syllable (e.g. H – his). Alongside these, there is the opening repetition of letters, perhaps his inventory of familiar letters. Interestingly, Christopher uses mainly upper-case letters. Many children will 'copy' their teacher's writing, but will convert classroom lower case print into upper case – a strategy which reinforces the argument that children rarely imitate

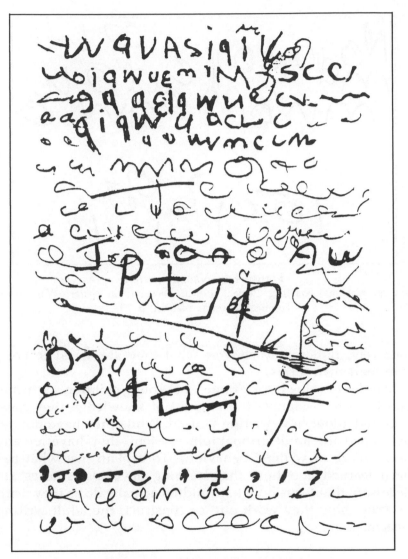

Figure 4.3 *Saiqa 'café' notebook.*
Source: National Writing Project 1989a: *Becoming a Writer*. Walton-on-Thames: Thomas Nelson, p. 72.

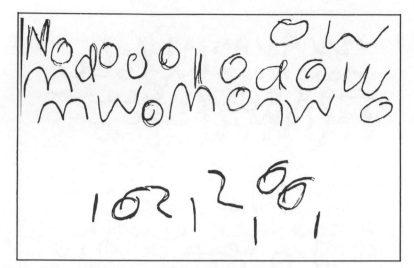

Figure 4.4   *Naomi's letter.*
Source: National Writing Project 1989a: *Becoming a Writer*. Walton-on-Thames: Thomas Nelson, p. 73.

passively, rather they convert what they are asked to copy into their own terms.

In order to value these examples of young children's writing, you have to recognize the amount of knowledge they have acquired about how writing is used. While they have not yet developed the adult orthographic system, they have already made sense of writers' behaviour. To explain just what has been learned and how that learning develops, studies are necessary that focus on what children actually do as they learn to write, how they work out, or construct, the adult writing system.

A psychological perspective

A major study of children's writing development that tried to do this was carried out by two Piagetian researchers, Ferreiro and Teberosky (1979, translated 1982). In the Piagetian tra-

Figure 4.5   *Christopher's experiments with writing. 'The Hulk is standing on a snake and Batman has got his pole.'*
Source: National Writing Project: unpublished child's text.

dition, the child is seen as the central agent in the analysis.
Development is interpreted from the point of view of the
learner; the theory has to fit what the child says or does, not
the other way round. The question of how children learn to
write can only be answered, from this psychological perspective, by looking at the paths children follow when they are
working out the characteristics, values and functions of written language. Ferreiro and Teberosky's starting point is as
follows:

We have searched unsuccessfully in the literature for references to
children themselves, thinking children who seek knowledge, children we have discovered through Piagetian theory. The children we
know through this theory are learners who actively try to understand
the world around them, to answer questions the world poses. They

are not learners who wait for someone to transmit knowledge to them in an act of benevolence. To the contrary, they learn primarily through their own actions on external objects, and they construct their own categories of thought while organising their world. (1982, p. 12)

Ferreiro and Teberosky could not believe that the child born surrounded by literacy would fail to make any sense of the printed world until she arrived at school. Knowing as we do the way a three-year-old will be asking the most difficult-to-answer questions; and knowing the way that a two-year-old can fashion language in the most inventive ways to express her needs, it would indeed be surprising if young children had totally ignored such a salient part of their world as writing.

Ferreiro and Teberosky's work involved giving children aged four to seven a number of reading and writing tasks. The tasks were introduced during flexibly structured interviews and, for the 'writing' study, involved asking the children to write their own names, the names of family members or friends, familiar words, less familiar words and a test sentence. Children were also asked to demonstrate their awareness of the difference between drawing and writing. From the children's responses, it was clear that children were actively constructing knowledge about writing, drawing on their experience of the world in general and on specific information transmitted to them about writing. Ferreiro and Teberosky suggested that children progress through a number of levels of literacy knowledge. Each level is identified by particular hypotheses held about the nature of reading and writing.

An early hypothesis about writing held by the youngest children is that there is a correspondence between their writing and the size of the object to be represented. So, one four-year-old claimed that the word for 'bear' would be bigger than the word for 'duck' because bears are bigger than ducks. Similarly, one girl said 'Write my name. But you have to make it longer because yesterday was my birthday'. Alongside such thinking are the children's notions about what could constitute a word. Many children stated that words should have a certain number of graphic characters (letter shapes were not always established at this point). Most insisted that a word has to have at least three characters (which, as was noted in chapter 3, most words do). Such conceptions of the length of written words Ferreiro and Teberosky classified as level 1. At this level, the children have not begun to analyse the graphic strings but are trying to relate writing to their knowledge of the rest of the world.

At the next level, the central hypothesis held by children is that there must be a different written form for different objects. This notion often coexists with the early hypothesis that each word must have a minimum number of characters. At the same time graphic forms become more letter-like. Combined, these new rules lead to writing in which a limited stock of characters is reordered to make different words. Thus, Martin wrote the requested words and sentence:

> MINMA = toad
> MIMIT   = duck
> OTIM   = bear
> OTMN   = rabbit
> MILTE   = my little girl sits in the
>   sun

(Note how many letters are from his own name.)

At level 3, a qualitative leap in thinking happens when children begin to assume that each letter represents a word or syllable, though they may not be consistent about which letter represents which syllable. This 'syllabic hypothesis' marks a significant point at which the child is analysing the whole representation into its parts and also beginning to make sound:symbol correspondences. But conflicts emerge here, conflicts that the researchers see as necessary to develop children's thinking one step further. One dilemma facing children is the development of a syllabic hypothesis alongside their learning of certain specific words such as their own names and those of their family, which do not follow the one letter = one syllable rule. A second conflict comes from the coexistence of a syllabic rule with the earlier theory that each word has a fixed number of letters. The child who wants to use four letters for each word will find that she does not need all four to represent the syllables: some letters will be left 'unread'. These tensions, Ferreiro and Teberosky argue, lead to the development of the alphabetic principle at level 4. This new level builds on or coexists with earlier ones and examples show the combination of hypothesis about fixed length, and syllabic and alphabetic principles. Gerardo, age six, writes:

MCA = mesa (table)
MAP = mapa (map)
PAL = palo (stick)

From the resolution of these conflicts by the child's internal restructuring of knowledge, supported only partly by adult intervention, children reach level 5 where the alphabetic principle is established. For Ferreiro and Teberosky, while much has still to be learned beyond this level, children 'do not have writing problems in the strict sense'. Conceptually, they have constructed the writing system.

The Ferreiro and Teberosky study represents one of the largest scale observations of young children's perceptions of literacy. (In addition to the questions asked about writing briefly summarized here, the researchers also studied children's awareness of print and their knowledge of reading.) It can be criticized for its experimental techniques which meant that the samples of writing analysed were very limited, with no examples of children's unaided or unprompted writing. This may have artificially restricted children's ability to show what they knew about writing and perhaps, as a result, led to a clearer delineation of levels of development than is actually the case. Other studies (e.g. Bissex, 1980) suggest that, when collections are made of children's spontaneous writing, while the principles identified by Ferreiro and Teberosky are evident, not all children seem to follow the same developmental path, and the distinctions between the levels are very blurred.

The importance of the child's first name

Notable in many of the examples of early writing is the use of letters from children's own first names. This is very common in children's early writing, perhaps not surprisingly when first names are so often pointed out to children by adults, and put on all their work, on their clothes, on their nursery pegs and so on. Ferreiro and Teberosky consider knowledge of the spelling of own names a significant factor in the development of writing as it creates major conflicts for the child at the different levels. For example, it can contradict the child's rule about the required number of letters for words; and it will be in conflict with a syllabic principle. It is through the coexistence of contradictory rules that, they argue, restructuring of knowledge takes place and a new level of learning is reached.

The argument about the significance of first name knowledge goes further than this and is worth a brief discussion. Gelb (1963), quoted in Ferreiro and Teberosky (1982, pp. 212–13), argues that the writing of proper names played a critical role in the historical development of alphabetic writing systems. Logographic systems, he argues, were not well suited to the representation of proper names, particularly for those in large urban areas, such as in Sumer, where, unlike in tribal communities, names were not unique to individuals, and where names could not adequately be represented by pictures (cf. Indian tribal names such as White-Buffalo). Phoneticization may well, therefore, have begun with proper names and from there spread to the whole of the system (remembering, of course, that not all languages use the alphabetic system and that even in English logographic and syllabic systems coexist with the dominant alphabetic one).

Gelb's argument does lead to an interesting discussion about the similarities between the conflicts that have faced communities developing effective systems of written communication and those facing young children struggling with their society's writing system. It is dangerous, of course, to read too much into the parallels between the historical development of the writing system and the individual child's development of writing. But one conclusion worth drawing is that a necessary condition for writing to develop is for individuals to be reflecting actively on language processes. We develop ways of using the system not simply by observing how others are using the system but by exploring new hypotheses and becoming aware of the fundamental properties of language. Put another way, development in writing takes place not only by learning how to use the system, but also learning about the system, a conceptual knowing. Karmiloff-Smith (1979, p. 2), in her studies of oral language development, talks about 'language as an object of the child's spontaneous cognitive attention, i.e. language as a problem-space per se'. Children, in other words, are not mere empiricists, observing what is around them and slowly acquiring the system; neither are they driven by some unfolding mechanism determining particular pathways of development. Instead, they are best viewed as learners who experiment, reflect, devise new solutions, refine ideas and move towards the adult system.

One example of a child's writing will illustrate what 'cognitive attention' to the writing system seems to involve. A four-year-old, quoted in Temple et al. (1982, p. 1), wrote:

YUTS A LADE YET FEHEG AD HE KOT FLEPR
Once a lady went fishing and she caught Flipper

Experienced readers of children's invented writing will be able to interpret the child's conceptualization of the writing system. There is her use of letter-name knowledge to find a letter to represent a sound; hence, Y (letter name *wy*) is used for the initial sound of 'once' and 'went'; similarly, E and R are used at the end of 'lady' and 'Flipper', perhaps on the grounds that their letter names represent the final syllables; interestingly, all nasals – Ns in 'went', 'fishing' and 'and' – are omitted, perhaps they are thought to be part of the vowel. This guesswork about the child's reasoning could continue. Suffice to show here that the child is using a system, her own, based on her experiences and supported by her instruction in writing.

Learning what writing is for

The emphasis, so far, has been on how children learn the writing system: the symbols, their order in words and their relationship to sounds. But this is only part of the learning process. Children are learning the system in order to do things with writing: to write lists, to take messages, to develop stories, to label and so on. While we can analyse all the examples above in terms of children's acquisition of the rules of writing, we can also see how they have learned to use writing for different purposes.

We need to look at how children have learned about writing events as well as about systems. Yetta Goodman (1988) makes this point when she identifies three overlapping principles controlling writing development that have separate roots: the functional, linguistic and relational principles. The functional principles refer to the child's knowledge about how writing is used, the different sorts of literacy events that people around them engage in. In Goodman's samples of writing she found children using writing for such functions as: controlling the behaviour of others (e.g. warning messages on doors); personal and interpersonal communication (e.g. labelling pictures and writing letters); representing experiences (e.g. story writing); explaining (e.g. writing about pictures or trips) and reminders (e.g. shopping lists). These categorizations, which do not seem to be mutually exclusive, must reflect the sociocultural context in which the child learns to write, a point expanded on below.

Goodman's other two principles are concerned with how the writing system works and thus supplement the work of Ferreiro and Teberosky and others. The linguistic principles go beyond a child's understanding of the orthographic system and include children's developing knowledge of the syntactic, semantic and pragmatic systems. Thus she highlights how children learn how different functions of writing require certain grammatical forms and text structures. Children learn that stories begin with phrases like 'Once upon a time' and that letters have openings such as 'Dear Granny'. Alongside these principles about the forms and functions of writing, Goodman adds a third relational principle which reflects children's developing awareness of how language represents the world. Examples she gives are of young children's attempts to work out how words represent objects (e.g. how size of object is related to length of word) and how sounds are represented by letters (e.g. such inventive spelling as that collected by Bissex (1980) 'EFU WAUTH KLOZ I WEL GEVUA WAUTHEN MATHEN: If you wash clothes I will give you a washing machine').

These principles are useful in extending the area of research from how a child learns about the system to how a child learns how it is used. The framework Goodman outlines provides a way of looking beyond the individual child as a logical problem-solver to a child as a collaborative learner working within a sociocultural context. One of my favourite examples of young children's writing which illustrates the collaborative nature of language learning comes from a Shropshire classroom involved in the National Writing Project (Czerniewska, 1988). Two reception class children, Fiona and Neil, were asked by their teacher, Sheila Hughes, to help each other write, once a week, starting with stories about their favourite colours. Fiona wrote her story herself with the teacher providing some spellings; Neil dictated his story for the teacher to write. Each text was accompanied by a picture. Once a week, they exchanged books and made comments which the teacher wrote underneath. As the weeks went by, their responses demonstrated an increasing awareness of the properties of writing and of each other's writing behaviour. These are some extracts:

Week 1

FIONA wrote:	I like black because I have toy black dog and I have always wanted a real life black dog.
NEIL commented:	She could have made it better if she'd put legs on the dog.
NEIL wrote:	I like yellow wallpaper and I am going to ask my dad if I can have some.

FIONA commented: He should have put 'wallpaper' at the end of his story.

Week 2

FIONA wrote: Red makes my mummy happy. She has a red Renault 5 car and there is a lot of room in the boot.

NEIL commented: She should have put spokes on the wheels and two lights front and back.

NEIL wrote: This a red lorry and I like it.

FIONA commented: He should have said where the lorry is going and why he liked it.

By week 6

FIONA wrote: The bear is trying to get some honey out of a tree. He looks very cuddly but really he is dangerous.

NEIL commented: Drawn a bigger tree. It is a good story.

NEIL wrote: My teddy bear is sitting by a tree thinking about doing something naughty.

FIONA commented: Ears and paws on the bear. I would like to know what naughty thing this teddy was going to do.

The children's responses to each other's texts reveal some of their knowledge about the functions of writing. Neil, for example, initially pays little attention to the words used and focuses on the accuracy of Fiona's picture. Fiona has clearer ideas about appropriate language structures. Her comment about the missing word 'wallpaper' is particularly interesting. Perhaps her assumption that 'wallpaper' is necessary at the end of the sentence reflects her experience of reading materials where there is a lot of repetition. As the weeks go by, both Fiona and Neil's writing become more complex and both appear affected by each other's comments. Neil starts to formulate more story-like texts, while Fiona starts paying more attention to her drawings. Their interaction illustrates for me the need to do more than describe a child's writing in terms of linguistic rules learned. We also need to consider the contexts in which writing is learned and how children learn about different literacy events.

The shift in thinking about early writing that has taken place is not simply a revision to the age at which writing behaviour first occurs, pushing the acquisition of writing back to the preschool years. It is not that researchers think it happens earlier but that they have radically questioned previous notions about the onset of literacy. Teale and Sulzby (1986) summarize what has been learned about literacy development in early childhood as follows:

1 Literacy development begins long before children start formal instruction. Children use legitimate reading and writing behaviours in the formal settings of home and community. The search for skills which predict subsequent achievement has been misguided because the onset of literacy has been misconceived.
2 *Literacy* development is the appropriate way to describe what was called *reading* readiness: the child develops as a *writer/reader*. The notion of reading preceding writing, or vice versa, is a misconception. Listening, speaking, reading and writing abilities (as aspects of language – both oral and written) develop concurrently and interrelatedly, rather than sequentially.
3 Literacy develops in real-life settings for real-life activities in order to 'get things done'. Therefore the functions of literacy are as integral a part of learning about writing and reading as are the forms of literacy.
4 Children are doing critical cognitive work in literacy development during the years from birth to six.
5 Children learn about language through active engagement with their world. They interact socially with adults in writing and reading situations; they explore print on their own, and they profit from modelling of literacy by significant adults, particularly their parents.
6 Although children's learning about literacy can be described in terms of generalized stages, children can pass through these stages in a variety of ways and at different ages. Any attempts to 'scope and sequence' instruction should take this developmental variation into account. (Quoted in Mercer, 1988, p. 259)

Teale and Sulzby use the word 'emergent' literacy to capture the significant aspects of recent models of writing and reading development. It signifies, they argue, development not stasis, where children are *in the process of becoming* literate. They are not pre- anything nor at stage zero in some developmental sequence.

Underlying these points is the critical argument that writing is not a series of skills that develop through informal support at home and formal instruction at school. Furthermore, acquisition is not solely dependent on the intellectual and physical maturation, i.e. the 'readiness' paradigm. Such a horticultural model (where abilities unfold at predictable times, nurtured by the environment) has been replaced by one in which the child actively participates in the language around her, using language-processing abilities to learn what it means to be a speaker, reader and writer in the community in which she lives.

Contexts for development

Teale and Sulzby, along with most of the research studies referred to above, centre on the individual child. Reference is made to the role of the environment and of significant adults in providing information about what writing looks like, how writers behave and how written language is used. But in most cases the image that is created is of the child working out the principles on her own, developing a unique system, albeit one that has much in common with other children's systems. But such a picture does not seem quite adequate to explain the child's learning processes. As Bruner puts it, children are not on solo flights mastering a set of skills but are involved in a collaborative venture:

I have come increasingly to recognise that most learning in most settings is a communal activity, a sharing of the culture. It is not just that the child must make his knowledge his own, but that he must make it his own in a community of those who share his sense of culture. It is this that leads me to emphasise not only discovery and invention but the importance of negotiation and sharing. (Bruner, 1986, p. 127)

In order to understand fully how children develop as writers we need to study the sociocultural contexts in which they learn to produce texts. This is a point already forcefully made in Heath's and others' work on uses of literacy in different communities (see chapter 1). When children are seen as constructing writing behaviour within particular social contexts, then paths of development begin to be questioned in new ways. We can ask whether a developmental sequence observed for a large number of children is a 'natural' occurrence or whether it has been negotiated through interaction with others. Such a perspective may highlight differences between groups according to their interactional histories: differences that may be very significant if they should fail to match the dominant educational expectations about development.

One small classroom-based study by Maclure (1986) illustrates how the sense children make of the writing system's forms and functions develops through a process of negotiation with those around them. Maclure begins with an observation, familiar to all Infants' teachers, that the early texts that five and six-year-old children produce to accompany their pictures are all broadly similar, such as

> This is my house. It is nice
> I am painting my house with my daddy

Characteristically, they are short, syntactically simple, without subordination. One possibility to account for the similarity among children's initial texts is that they reflect some specific constraint on children's ability to write more complex texts. This clearly cannot be due to general language maturity as children's oral language at this age is far more complex syntactically and semantically. However, it could be argued (as claimed by Kress, 1982) that written language presents new and different language problems for children, causing a disparity between their oral and written production in terms of

complexity. Against this view is the evidence from samples
of children's writing in different contexts, particularly those
where invented spellings are actively encouraged, which demonstrate that children can, in certain contexts, generate written
texts of considerable linguistic complexity. For example, one
nursery child wrote in his personal journal the linguistically
sophisticated message shown in figure 4.6.

To try to explain the similarities between the classroom-
produced texts, Maclure looked at the effect of the schooling

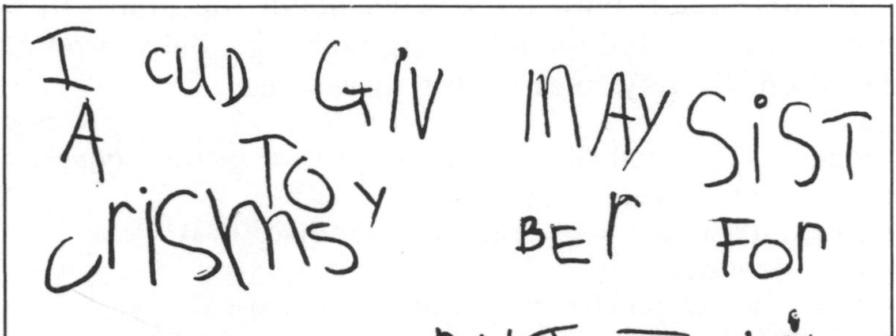

Figure 4.6 *A nursery child's message in his journal. 'I could give my
sister a toy bear for Christmas but I will have to hide it. I could hide it
in the bed or under the bed.'*
Source: National Writing Project 1989a: *Becoming a Writer*. Walton-on-
Thames: Thomas Nelson, p. 86.

process itself. She suggests that it is the interactional strategies that teachers adopt that shape young children's writing. The social context she studied was the 'negotiation' that happens between teacher and child about to write under the child's picture, in the typical literacy event of 'draw a picture, then compose a caption for it'. By analysing the interactions of teacher and child during the collaborative composing of the captions she found that certain types of written texts were being constructed. One example demonstrates an interactional style that she found was commonly practised.

During the drawing of her picture, Betty engaged in a lengthy discussion with the teacher about the house in her picture. At the end of the following exchange, Betty produced the caption: 'Nanny lives in this nice house'.

TEACHER: . . . what shall we write about your picture today?
BETTY: nice house
TEACHER: it's a nice house yes. and who lives in it?
BETTY: nanny
TEACHER: nanny. ( ) shall we write nanny lives
                              in
BETTY: in uh her house
TEACHER: this nice – ?
BETTY: house
TEACHER: house. all right.

The teachers that Maclure observed were not actually doing all the transcribing; in some cases their interventions were very minor. But the negotiation of what constitutes a text tended to encourage simple sentences of a certain length and syntactic pattern. With older children, a second sentence was encouraged but with little opportunity provided for subordination or use of connectives. To summarize Maclure's conclusions, the teachers appeared to be framing, through their questions and responses, the children's writing into a narrow range of language options. The interaction may well have value in encouraging children to use their own language as the basis of their writing (an argument underlying the valued 'language experience' approach) but it may be that what appears to be the child's own language is, in effect, a classroom-made language. The cost of such interactions may be a lack of experimentation with other forms/functions of writing. Maclure would go further in her argument and suggest that the interactional strategies reflect discourse practices which are typical of teacher–pupil talk across the curriculum and throughout the school years.

These discourse structures reflect (and reenact) the 'asymmetry' of knowledge and status which usually exists between adults and children in general. This suggests that the ways in which teachers interact with pupils during writing sessions are not just the outcome of 'preferences' for approaching writing one way or another: they may also reflect more general constraints placed on teachers and children by the social organisation and prevailing views of children as learners. (Maclure, 1986, pp. 9–10)

Any account, model or set of curriculum guidelines for writing needs to acknowledge the role played by the learner in language construction. Language cannot be viewed simply as a body of knowledge which can be split into smaller nuggets according to the size of the child. Children come to the language tasks set by school with considerable knowledge about written forms and functions through their active explorations of the language around them. Within schools, the writing a child develops is the result of the interactions between the teacher, child and the task. The next chapter looks at ways in which the writing environment of the classroom is constructed.

5

Writing in the Classroom

Two strong messages have emerged from studies of children's writing development and theories of the meaning of literacy. The first is that literacy is not a static concept, its definition varies over time and between cultures. Literacy is not some monolithic language medium, definable and teachable as a set of skills. On the contrary, literacy needs to be seen as a set of social practices, functional varieties of language which are drawn on according to the purposes and audiences found in a particular social context. Teachers of literacy need always to be asking themselves about the view of literacy they are promoting. Does the view support or conflict with the literacy practices of a child's home culture? And do the different types of writing taught in school equip children to cope confidently with the different functions of literacy that they will face when they leave school? Arguably, current practices in the teaching of writing are not adapting to the new dimensions of literacy brought about by technological innovations nor are they confronting the issue that today literacy does not necessarily equate with getting a job. (See Spencer, 1986, for a discussion of 'emergent literacies').

The second and related message evident from a close look at young children's writing is that children are active participants in the process of literacy development. Children learn to read and write not by assimilating a body of adult knowledge, but by actively working out how the writing system is organized and used. Furthermore, this process of construction happens in interaction with others. Children learning to be literate are involved in a collaborative venture with others of their culture.

The recognition that literacy has diverse, context-dependent functions and outcomes and that children are actively involved in making sense of that functional diversity underpins many current approaches to the teaching of writing. My aim here is to try to describe, and to evaluate, some of the approaches to the teaching of writing that teachers have been developing over the past ten years or so, drawing heavily on the work of the hundreds of schools involved in the National Writing Project (1985–9). At the same time, I want to identify some major theoretical frameworks that underlie such practice. Theory is much neater than practice, and in any one curriculum you can identify classroom practices drawing from a number of different theoretical perspectives. However, in order to provide an account of the teaching of writing that can best inform those involved in curriculum development, and that can lead to evaluation and change of current practice, it seems best to start by looking not at the theory but at the less neat classroom.

Starting with practice

The way of looking at current practice adopted by teachers around the country in the National Writing Project was one that made certain assumptions about learning and learners. In essence, the belief was that learning is affected by the ways in which the curriculum organizes information and the ways in which abilities are defined and measured. The nature of the interaction with children affects both what is learned and how well it is learned. With this interactional perspective, it follows that learning to write is not just a question of being exposed to instruction about writing. Writing development takes place through a complex interaction involving teachers, pupils and the curriculum. To explore these interactions we can ask questions such as:

1   How is the task of writing presented to children? Is
it something to be done after an event, such as a
school outing or a science experiment? Is it something
to be done alone and in silence? Is it something that
always gets finished by the end of the lesson? Is it
always for the teacher?

2   How is writing represented in different subject areas?
Are certain types of writing reserved for different
subject areas. Are narratives only found in English;
reports only for science; and fill-in-the-blank exercises
for geography? What does a whole week's worth of
writing look like in terms of the range of writing
varieties experienced?

3   What do children think is important in writing? Neat-
ness? Spelling? Knowledge of a range of written varieties?

4   How do children evaluate their abilities? What sense
do they have of their own development as writers
during the composition of one text and during the
course of a term or year?

5   What do children know about writing and writers?
Who do they see write? Their teacher? Their parents?
What do they know about the stages in the production
of a text?

To find some answers to these questions, teachers, children
and researchers have looked at the writing 'diet' of children
by asking teachers to keep records of all writing tasks and by
collecting writing samples of all the writing done in a given
time period by children in a particular group of schools.
Alongside these data about written 'output', teachers have
explored children's perceptions of the writing task and of
themselves as writers through interviews, journals and ques-
tionnaires (see NWP, 1990b). Schools across the country have
logged their writing curriculum in various ways but, despite
the different procedures used, findings have shown a remarkable degree of consensus. Some of the main points which
caused teachers to think hard about the writing curriculum
that was being delivered were:

1 **Technical accuracy and speed are most highly valued**
A survey of children in a Durham primary school provided these typical responses to the question 'Are you a good writer?':
Bad – my spellings are wrong.
Nearly – I would be much better if I was faster.
No – too scribbly.
To be a good writer you have to be a good speller.
To be a good writer you have to be neat, careful and quite quick.

2 **The importance of writing is often defined in terms of future needs**
Asked 'Why do we learn to write?' pupils said:
People write so they can get a job. We write to help us learn and get a job so we can make money.
So we are ready to go in the juniors.
To write letters when you grow up.
To write reports when you grow up.

3 **Reasons for writing often centre around some general communication function**
Some Dorset and Avon ten and eleven-year-olds' views reflected those of their peers around the country:
I think we write because it is another way of communicating with one another.
I like to write because you can write to people you like.
(We write) so we can communicate with each other.
Some go further:
Writing can be for many different reasons like these . . . to be read, to express your feelings, to tell people things, to say what you feel and to express other people's feelings as well as your own. Writing is a type of communication.
Others seems content to have no communicative purpose:
I like writing because if you did not write you would have nothing to do all day in school.
Children write to do their work at school.

Writing is for you to be able to know more words and to do neater writing.

4   A most frequently mentioned 'audience' for writing is the teacher

Writing shows your teacher how you are progressing.

I write for my teacher to prove I can write.

What you write is up to you when you are at home, and if you are at school it is up to the teacher what you write about.

Sometimes we write so that the teacher knows what we are thinking.

5   Writers are identified as a rather special section of the community

(teachers are not classed as writers themselves)

I think that writers should be middle aged and they should be calm.

A writer does not only write he/she does the things normal people do.

Some people don't just write some are very active and do a lot of sport. Or others just relax at home thinking about their books and getting fat.

As more children were asked about their perceptions of writing, a picture emerged of enthusiastic writers (most children seemed to enjoy writing) who saw the main function of writing in school as teaching them how to write. While 'communication' figured as a reason for writing, specific purposes for writing were rarely acknowledged beyond those that satisfied the teacher-defined tasks. Writing was rarely mentioned as a tool for the child's own learning. The reader for children's writing was usually identified as the teacher. Children's success in this learning process was judged by them mainly in terms of their control over the orthographic system. Once technically accomplished, they assumed that the way was open to a job and a future of writing reports and letters. While many of these observations are welcome, they disappointed some teachers who hoped that children saw writing as important for their immediate personal and learning needs, not simply as a means to some future end.

The responses draw attention to the ways in which children make sense of school activities, ways that have not always been intended by their teachers. The children's perceptions demonstrate that writing activities cannot be separated from the context in which they occur. Whenever a teacher asks for some writing to be done, the writing produced will be affected not just by the task at hand but by the shared understandings about writing in that classroom. So, for example, a task such as writing a letter is going to be perceived differently by pupils according to the understandings that have developed about the task: understandings about who determines the content and the style; about the collaboration allowed; about the importance of layout; about what paper is used, and about what happens to the letter – is it put into an exercise book, mounted on the wall or actually sent? For any writing task there is a context of shared meanings that is constructed mentally by the pupils and the teacher about the task's intended purpose and audience. Edwards and Mercer (1987) refer to the set of educational 'ground rules' that develop in schools through the interaction of child, teacher and task.

To explore further the nature of the contextual framework in which children work out the 'ground rules' of writing, questions can be asked such as: what happens to a piece of writing when it's finished? Does it get sent somewhere? Shown to its potential readership? Put on display? What writing gets puts up on the wall – the neatest writer's? The teacher-corrected version? Who puts it up there and at whose eye level is it? Who decides what the writing task is? How often is the purpose for writing negotiated between the teacher and the pupils? Does everyone do exactly the same writing task at the same time? Does every writing task lead to a finished 'product'?

Questions are many and each answer helps to form a picture of the way writing is being defined by the teacher and by the children. What emerges from observations of the classroom is not simply a description of the physical conditions under which learning takes place (though these are important) but an understanding of the system of shared meanings about writing that has been created between teachers and children.

For example, some Manchester nursery teachers observed the writing environments they had created and noted, among other things, that all the writing up on the nursery wall had been written by the teacher, mounted and put up by the teacher and placed at adult eye level (NWP, 1989a). They used these observations to discuss the messages that were invoked by, or constructed from, that environment; messages about the kind of writing that was valued (e.g. neat, correctly spelled adult writing), the functions that it served (e.g. to display to other adults what had been done in class) and about who controlled what was written, when and by whom.

The teachers who were asking and answering these questions about classroom practices in the teaching of writing were not satisfied by what they found. They discovered restrictions that were being placed on children's writing not from any direct instructional content of lessons but from the subtle messages created within their classrooms. One Manchester teacher wrote:

My classroom was full of labels and written instructions, but I was suddenly aware that they were for my benefit as a teacher and they were what should be there; they 'looked right'. The children had no sense of ownership and so their writing was of little value. (NWP, 1989a, p. 30)

Similarly, another group of teachers raised an important issue about whose writing was being valued:

A point we raised was the question of how much print should be in minority languages. We also felt we had to demonstrate to the children that we valued and respected their language and culture by commenting on the different scripts and styles, rather than simply displaying lots of captions from different languages with no comments made. (NWP, 1989a, p. 30)

From these explorations of actual writing practices in classrooms there developed a whole rethink about the organization of the classroom and the curriculum. Different strategies began to be discussed and implemented and new approaches to the teaching of writing began to be formulated. Many of the ideas were not new. What was often new was the reformulation about how the writing task should be negotiated between children and teachers.

A 'process' approach to writing

One approach to the writing curriculum seemed to provide just the type of orientation to learning and to writing that would free children from the burdens of skill acquisition and allow them to explore the richness and diversity of written language. This is generally called the 'process' approach, though under that term are identifiably different frameworks for viewing writing. It might be better to think not of one approach but of a general 'movement' with all that such a term entails in terms of followers, converts and heretics. It is a movement that has swept across the United States and Australia, and to some extent the United Kingdom (though here the British reserve seems to have dampened some of the fervour seen in other countries). It remains highly influential, as can be seen in the place it holds in National Curriculum documents for English.

The process approach reflects a shift in thinking away from the products of writing towards the processes of writing and from the text to the writer. The focus is on how we can help children understand and engage in the act of writing, how they use writing in different ways and how well they can discuss how writing differs according to its use and readership. The emphasis of the approach is on writing as a set of behaviours which can be learned, talked about and developed in different situations. As Cooper (1986) points out, this shift has its parallel in current emphases in reading instruction on the way readers interpret texts, bringing to the act of reading a body of knowledge and a set of values and attitudes that determine how the text is read. Young writers and readers are seen as bringing to texts expectations and interpretive strategies. This mental equipment needs to develop not through exercises in word recognition and spelling but through writing that uses knowledge from literacy events.

At the core of the process movement, spearheaded by the work of the US researchers Donald Graves and Donald Murray in particular, is an analysis of writing as a series of stages each with a distinctive type of behaviour. One popular model represents writing as having five stages: pre-writing, drafting, revision, editing, publishing. The terms and number of stages differ between writers; for example, Murray (1984) has a circular model with five stages labelled: collect, focus, order, draft, clarify. But despite these differences, there remains the essential focus on the complex set of writer's operations involved in a text's production. All process theorists stress that the stages in the writing process are recursive rather than linear. So, for example, after an initial draft, the writer may return to pre-writing behaviours such as discussion and note-taking, or during editing the writer may carry out further drafting etc. It is intended as a dynamic process, though once institutionalized as classroom practice, the process risks becoming static. As Cooper (1986) puts it, 'revolution dwindles to dogma'.

The process model of writing contrasts markedly with the one-off writing procedures that so many pupils experience, and it is a model that has immediate intuitive appeal to all adults who write (or avoid writing). For each stage, we can identify different strategies we use. The pre-writing stage is a familiar one. It is identifiable by behaviours such as talking around a subject with colleagues or friends, opening books for inspiration, jotting down ideas on the backs of envelopes or having an uncontrollable urge to do the ironing. Once drafting begins there are all the false starts, the worries about the right tone to adopt, the screwed up paper in the bin and, eventually, something that looks as though it might be right. Then comes revision which may involve someone else reading what you have written – that can be painful. Then more drafts if you can face it and think it worth while. Finally, the polishing up can start, and the typing or rewrite, as appropriate. Then it can be sent, published, stuck on the wall or end up in whatever form it was designed for.

Discussion of the writing process often allows us to identify where we have particular problems – personally, I put off revision for a long time – and we can talk about the pleasures and the pains, both mental and physical, that writing brings with it. Perhaps the most illuminating in-service sessions on writing that I have been involved in have asked teachers to talk about how they feel as writers, how often they write, how they hate or love writing, and, importantly, how often they talk about and demonstrate the writing process in front of their pupils.

For many teachers, this recognition and articulation of what a writer does provides an answer to some of the dissatisfactions of past practice. Writing comes to be seen as much more than a set of skills taught through exercises. The writer (whether child or adult) can be viewed as someone facing real problems that will not simply disappear once inspired inner voices are conjured up. Writing is recognized as a craft, and the teacher, as the more experienced craftsperson, has the role of introducing pupils to the craft know-how. Graves, one of the most seductive writers in the history of writing pedagogy puts it like this:

We don't find many teachers of oil painting, piano, ceramics or drama who are not practitioners in their fields. Their students see them in action in the studio. They can't teach without showing what they mean. There is a process to follow. There is a process to learn. That's the way it is with a craft, whether it be teaching or writing. There is a road to travel, and there is someone to travel with us, someone who has already made the trip . . . A craft is a process of shaping material toward an end. There is a long painstaking, patient process demanded to learn how to shape the material to a level where it is satisfying to the person doing the crafting. Both craft processes, writing and teaching, demand constant revision, constant reseeing of what is being revealed by the information in hand; in one instance the subject of the writing, in another the person learning to write. The craftsperson is a master follower, observer, listener, waiting to catch the shape of the information. (Graves, 1983, p. 6)

Graves shows, with many practical examples, just how the painstaking, patient process of shaping can be enacted in the classroom, through specific organizational strategies such as 'writer's conferences', teachers modelling the process, book-binding and publication. He (and others) present both a theory of how writers think while writing and also classroom practices through which such cognitive behaviours can be developed.

An extract from an account of work in an Avon Junior classroom by Vera Pelley illustrates how examination of the writing process translated into her classroom practice (a full account is in NWP, 1989c, p. 52–56):

Over the last few years I had looked at the question of audience, and from time to time we had written pieces for children of different ages and parents as well as 'business letters'. I had looked carefully at the preparation for writing and had provided the opportunity for children to work in rough before the final copy. The children always wrote on paper so that their work could be made into a book at the end of the school year.

The system seemed to be working quite well, within its limitations, but all the time I had the distinct feeling that I wasn't doing enough to extend and clarify the children's ideas, sharpen up their use of language or improve their presentation. Time always seemed to be against me. To allow time for each child to read a story to me and then discuss it in detail would have required many uninterrupted hours each week. So, on the whole what happened was that spelling and punctuation were put right by various methods, content was usually left alone if it was reasonable and we concentrated on getting a good neat final copy.

Now that we work through the processes of drafting, editing and publishing, I feel that the finished work is more satisfying for the children, and, moreover, they find the process more interesting. They have a heightened awareness of the stages through which an idea passes to become a piece of published work; they enjoy the opportunity to collaborate with others; they share success with each other.

Our new way of working started when we did a short topic on both books and authors. We looked at different types of books, different bindings, covers, print and paper. We talked about the work of authors, editors, printers, publishers and illustrators. The question 'What is an author?' helped them to regard their own work in a new light.

The children were now introduced to the idea of drafting – writing only on every other line, with spelling unimportant at this stage. For four weeks, the children wrote weekly first drafts without following them up. One was a piece of writing about pocket money, another was a story written for younger children, the third was an adventure story and for the fourth piece they had a free choice of subject. Each week, I read the drafts and wrote questions and/or comments such as:

> Why did Sam think the dog was fierce?
> I can't imagine what sort of girl Sarah is – can you tell me about her?

At the end of the four weeks I asked the children to read through the four pieces of work and my comments on them, and then choose one draft they would like to continue with and eventually make into a book. Almost all chose the story they had written for younger children.

The development of their storybooks then followed a particular sequence which, in summary, included:

1 Class discussion
2 First draft (the teacher also wrote one)
3 Revision (modelled first by looking at the teacher's draft)
4 Second draft (not necessarily a rewrite)
5 Consulting (in groups of three, children read and commented on drafts)
6 Third (usually final) draft
7 Editing (detailed correction, mainly of spelling and punctuation)
8 Preparation for publication (including layout and instructions for typist)
9 Illustrations
10 The cover
11 Binding
12 Reading the finished books to their audience

Vera Pelley comments on the effects of the approach:

The atmosphere in the classroom is very much that of a workshop. One group may be editing, another illustrating, another writing a final copy. There is an encouraging air of industry and enthusiasm

about the whole process. . . . One day I asked the children to write
a comment on drafting and editing in their journals: 'I like doing
drafts about stories because when you are doing your second draft
you can get different ideas and make your story better. I like to do
about three drafts because you usually find that your story gets
better and better every time. I think the editing was a very good
idea. I like it because it made the story better because people find
mistakes and if you miss a fault they might see it. I think editing
made the story better' (Richard).

This account captures the type of writing activity that
occurred in many classrooms influenced by the process model.
For many, such as Vera Pelley, the change was not very great
organizationally, children already worked in groups and were
used to a variety of writing tasks. What was new was the shift
in focus away from the finished text and towards how that
text was produced. Children found themselves learning a
whole new vocabulary and began talking about 'drafting',
'proofreading' and 'layouts'. The techniques introduced were
very detailed and 'professional'. For instance, at the editing
stage, these nine and ten-year-olds were taught a number of
editing symbols such as those to mark omissions and deletions
as well as noting spelling errors. The children are being seen
as authors and writing is being seen as a craft with its own
methods that can be passed on from the more experienced
craftsperson (the teacher) to the less experienced.

Writing and personal expression

While there was something refreshingly new about the 'process' approach – some would argue that it was revolutionary,
a paradigm shift – it clearly sat quite comfortably on many
existing layers of practice. It maintained many of the arguments of the earlier 'personal growth' or 'expressive' movement which prevailed in the 1960s and early 1970s (e.g. Dixon,
1967; Elbow, 1973). This earlier framework for writing stressed
the value of integrity, creativity, spontaneity and individu-

ality. The teaching of writing was seen as a process of unlocking children's creative potential, of finding a real 'voice'. A quote from Elbow (1973) captures the feel of the approach:

Think of writing as an organic developmental process in which you start writing at the very beginning – before you know your meaning at all – and encourage your words gradually to change and develop. Only at the end will you know what you want to say or the words you want to say it with. (Quoted in Faigley, 1986)

Many teachers had become dissatisfied with aspects of this approach. Its 'horticultural' model of child development, in which the adult role was to provide a rich soil in which to watch the child bloom, did not seem enough when teachers faced children failing to write anything other than flat, uninteresting texts. It provided too few answers to problems about the children who did not develop beyond a basic under-standing of the orthographic system. Teachers often felt insecure about their role. To intervene in a child's writing might interfere with the natural growth of the child's creative potential; and yet not to intervene seemed to leave many children making little progress.

Despite the criticisms of the 'creative' approaches, there remained much sympathy to many of its basic tenets. There was much support for the central role given to the individual child in the learning process. Furthermore, many agreed with the notion that children should be provided with opportuni-ties to choose what they wrote about, and that they should be free to use writing to express their own feelings and beliefs. The 'process' approach which stresses the cognitive and behavioural aspects of writing combines well with deeply held notion about the 'expressive' aspects. The new process framework that developed was one in which writing could be taught as a craft, not simply left to emerge from within the child. Yet at the same time, children could have control over what they wrote and use writing to discover their own inner meanings. The two discourses of 'personal growth' and 'cogni-tive process' models fit well together; the teacher of 'process' has knowledge about how to write which can be passed on and yet she can remain loyal to views of personal expression, maintaining and promoting a view of the child as self-motivating and self-discovering. Cooper (1986) puts it like this:

The new model legitimated pedagogical methods many of us wanted to use or were using already. We could talk about ideas rather than forms in the classroom and could send students off to do various kinds of free writing and writing using heuristics in order to find out what they thought about a topic – and best of all, none of this writing was designed to be read by us. Students were given primary responsibility for the purpose of their writing: only they could decide what was important to them to write about, only they could tell whether what they intended was actually fulfilled in the writing they produced. (Cooper, 1986)

Classroom strategies took hold that were both strongly personal and at the same time reflective of the child's understanding about writing. Perhaps the best example of the interplay of these perspectives is in the highly successful introduction of journals to the writing classroom. Journals come in many forms and by many names. They have been variously called learning logs, diaries, 'think books' or scratch pads. They have been used as strictly private books, or as shared writing places for children, parents and teachers; used for reflection about specific learning problems or used for anything that comes to mind; for use at allotted times or for use any time; and so on. But, despite many differences, the use of journals shares an underlying assumption that children need a place 'outside' the recognized writing curriculum where they can play with writing and experiment with new forms. Journals are seen as places for personal expression, for 'free' writing which teachers do not assess. They provide opportunities for children to see that writing is more than communication of information and ideas, it also serves for exploration of thoughts and feelings. Journals can serve a further function by providing an 'off the record' place for dialogue with the teacher, a place where personal concerns about learning and progress can be voiced and where evaluation can be made about a lesson.

Many writing curricula were changed quite dramatically once teachers gave out journals to their class and saw what children would write and were able to write once their writing was unencumbered by traditional restrictions on content, organization and style. Two examples of journals in use illustrate some of the learning opportunities they offered.

Journals in a Dorset school provided a resource for both the children and the teacher, Elise Vear, to reflect on their thinking in ways not found in the standard 'write about what we did today' mode. During a study of the local river, the Juniors visited a local water mill and afterwards were asked to devise a water wheel from whatever material they thought appropriate. In their journals they recorded their ideas and feelings. Journals also gave these children a chance to write about events of immediate importance (figures 5.1, 5.2).

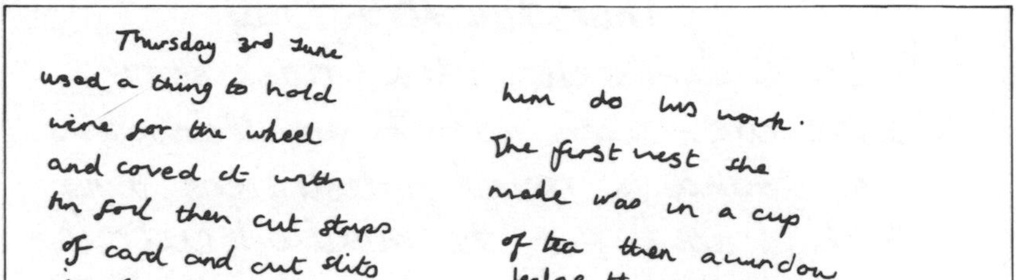
Thursday 3rd June
used a thing to hold
wire for the wheel
and coved it with
tin foil then cut strips
of card and cut slits
in them. Then I made
card bord squares
and ~~stuck~~ stuk them
in the slits.
"O" Mrs vear I want
to tell you about
a little robin
in a friends
work shop it
works with him
and sits on his
tools and watches
him do his work.
The first nest she
made was in a cup
of tea then a window
ledge then on top
of a pile of plastic
on a shelf ~~th~~ that
she uses on and
off all year
but at the ~~moment~~
moment she is in
a ~~umbell~~ umberella
with five eggs. when
we were there he tapped
the nest and she stuck
her head out and then
hopped onto the ~~p~~ perce
of wood

Thank you for the lovely description. They are fascinating aren't they – much more interesting than the water wheel!

Figure 5.1 *Journal writing on robins.*
Source: National Writing Project 1989b: *Writing and Learning*. Walton-on-Thames: Thomas Nelson, p. 45.

Our Water Wheels

Monday, 25th. May

I am thinking how to make it and what out of.

Tuesday, 26th, May

I am still thinking about it.

Wednesday, 27th, May

I am thinking about making the wheel we made at school.

Thursday, 28th, May

I have a different idea. I have some plastic egg cups which are transparent. I also found a round polestoryrene thing which I used for the middle. I cut out 8 egg cups but I could only stick on (with blue tap) 4. Then I stuck a pen through a hole in the centre I made with the pen. I took my water wheel to the sink and tried it. It would work a bit but the sink wasn't deep enough so I put it under the bath tap. like a charm the wheel whirled round. The tape though peeled off so I used a yellow material tape and it worked well.

Figure 5.2 Journal writing on 'Our Water Wheels'.
Source: National Writing Project 1989b: *Writing and Learning*. Walton-on-Thames: Thomas Nelson, p. 43.

Strategies for writing

The focus on the process of writing and on the writer rather than the text involves asking how writers behave when they write. What goes on in their heads? What mental strategies are used and how do these differ between the beginner and mature writer? Or between the 'good' and the 'poor' writer? Teachers began to look afresh at familiar complaints like 'they always write the same thing'/'the writing begins well but usually collapses half way through'/'when children redraft, nothing much changes apart from a few spelling errors.' Instead of assuming that such failings are the result of children's age or their lack of interest or ability, teachers began to see the issues as typical writer's problems which could be supported by specific strategies. New insights into children's writing patterns came not only from the powerful arguments of 'process' theorists and practitioners, but also from teachers' examination of their own writing. When you start talking about your own writing difficulties and successes, it doesn't take long before you realize that your comments parallel those of young children: the problems of facing the blank sheet of paper; the fatigue that sets in halfway through and so on.

To find out more about the mental processes that affect a writer's behaviour and to come up with answers that might help foster better writing, many educationists looked towards cognitive science. This branch of psychology provides some models of information-processing and some experimental methods that help us to understand the workings of the writer's mind. The methods have much in common with (and draw on) work on artificial intelligence that attempts to simulate human behaviour. Much of the representation of behaviour draws on computer analogies, with writing processes related to each other in flow charts, and the whole act of writing being pictured as a set of relatively simple cognitive operations that produce enormously complex actions (e.g. Flower and Hayes, 1980). One method, for example, has been to ask writers to talk about what they are thinking about as they write. From these statements researchers have generated writing 'protocols' which are then broken down into a series of goal-directed steps that draw on various cognitive processing strategies.

There are a number of major reservations to be made about the approach. It tends to neglect the content of writing and tends to view the writer as simply a text-generator, reducing him or her to a socially isolated operator of cognitive skills. There are reservations, too, about the methods of enquiry – can one ever find out what a writer thinks? Does the very act of thinking about what you are doing when writing change the process of writing itself? However, the work has made valuable contributions to our understanding of writing development by its focus on the types of cognitive demands that certain pedagogic approaches place on the young writer.

Two examples from the work of Scardamalia and Bereiter illustrate the direction of this line of enquiry into the writing process. They see the purpose of their studies as a means of understanding 'the internal problems that young writers must actually face in composition – the problems as they actually come to bear on the psychological system of the child trying to write' (Bereiter and Scardamalia, 1985). Their studies have centred on issues such as children's memory capacity and strategies for recalling information. How, for example, can children recall and organize all the information they have on a particular topic when they begin to write? One study (Bereiter and Scardamalia, 1985) asked ten and 12-year-olds to think of everything they knew about three familiar and three unfamiliar topics (a task that in itself proved taxing as children could not easily come up with the required number of topics). While children could think of more content items for familiar topics, the writing that they produced on the familiar and unfamiliar subjects was indistinguishable. It seemed that children first had difficulty with memory searches of the sort 'what do I know about X?' Secondly, even when they had identified things they knew, these did not provide enough content for writing. In the researchers' terms, the children had difficulty activating knowledge. Bereiter and Scardamalia put it this way:

For any complex writing task, the relevant knowledge is likely to be scattered among a variety of nodes. Unless the potentially useful nodes are brought up to a state of ready accessibility, goal directed search is likely to fail. (1985, p. 108)

These memory difficulties lead to the familiar writing problems faced by children (and adults): it is hard to think of a topic to write about, hard to find a starting point and, once a topic is begun, it is easy to run out of ideas. Bereiter and Scardamalia attribute such difficulties not to immature cognitive mechanisms but to children's lack of experience of generating language by themselves. Solo composing practices required for writing are far different from the conversations that children will have experienced. Conversations (dialogues might be a better term) are usually centred around familiar topics and are supported by what others are saying and by cues in the context. Such support helps to activate the right memory nodes. ('Sticky' conversations are probably rarely experienced by children.)

From such analysis, the researchers have looked at techniques used by teachers to support the writer struggling for content. Pre-writing activities such as class discussion of a topic or 'brainstorming' techniques seem potentially to offer ways of supporting the young writer, providing, in the researchers' terms, executive routines for carrying out effective memory searches. Strategies such as 'web'-making (figure 5.3) should help a child's current and future writing.

The researchers' experiments are based on hypothetical writing situations. Most teachers would avoid giving a child a blank piece of paper, a topic and the instruction 'write'. However, children are expected to generate language for themselves in activities where 'free' writing is valued or where children are encouraged to write under a very general heading such as 'News'. Barry Wade (1983) provides a nice example of what happens in such activities. 'Mark', a ten-year-old, reflects on his experiences of 'news time' in the Infants' school:

When I was in the Infants we used to have News every Monday morning and when we had finished talking about it we went off and wrote about it, and every Monday morning without fail I wrote,

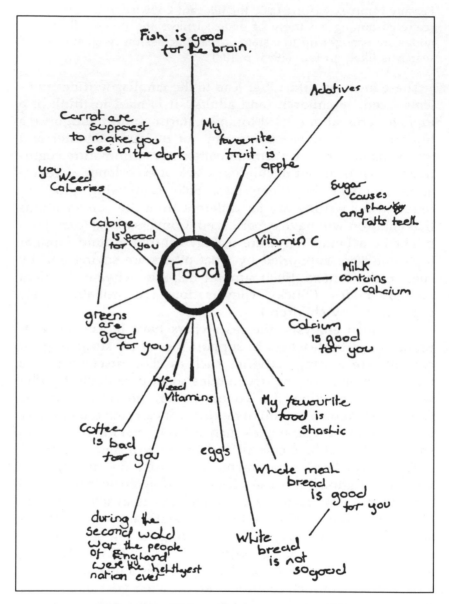

Figure 5.3   *Web-making to support writing.*
Source: National Writing Project 1989b: *Writing and Learning*. Walton-on-
Thames: Thomas Nelson, p. 10.

'I played football with my brother', or 'I went to my Nans', but one morning when I wrote 'I played football with my brother', my teacher said, 'I'm getting fed up with you writing the same things every morning, go away and write something different for a change.' 'Alright', I said. I went and wrote, 'I went to my Nans', and from then, I thought that I would write that every week when we had News. (Wade, 1983)

In a Hampshire classroom, the problem of seemingly stereo-typed 'News' was looked at closely by the teacher and Writing Project coordinator, Roger Mulley, supported by researcher, Margaret Axford. Their work paralleled that of Scardamalia and Bereiter in its focus on the writer's problems. They explained the context of their work thus:

An earlier examination of news-writing throughout the school had shown that young children often find it difficult to keep to a subject. As they come under increasing pressure to write more, they tend to accumulate several events rather than to develop one. Seven-year-old Michael's news is typical of the kind of chronological catalogue that results.

'On Saturday my cousin came to sleep with me and on Sunday we went to the Park Parade and the next day he slept again and in the morning we went out to play up the park and we went on the swings and then we went on the climbing frame to play up for touch.'

We wanted to see how children might be helped to focus their attention more sharply, and elaborate on specific ideas. (NWP, 1989a, p. 49)

The strategies they developed involved children selecting their favourite topics then collaboratively 'brainstorming' what they knew about a chosen subject. They were then shown how to group ideas into themes, and how to enlarge on statements through questions that would make their meanings more explicit. Talking, sharing and seeing the writing techniques modelled by the teacher were central to the work. And the strategies appeared to pay off in the children's writing which seemed to explore better the possibilities of the subject and to 'give greater scope for personal response'. Michael's text in the final session reflected the new way of working (figure 5.4).

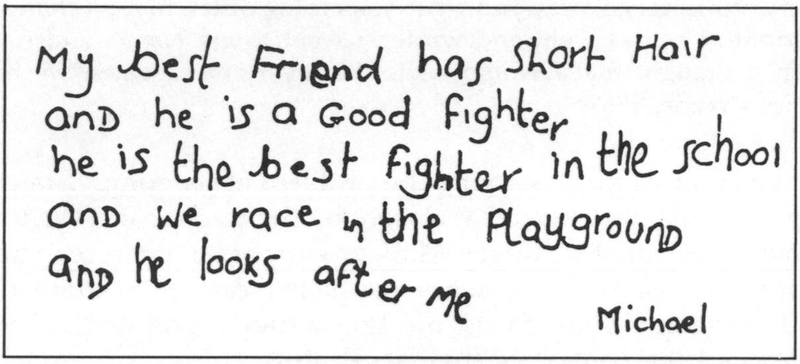

My best Friend has short Hair
and he is a Good fighter
he is the best fighter in the school
and we race in the Playground
and he looks after me
                              Michael

Figure 5.4   *Michael's text in the final session reflecting the new way of working.*
Source: National Writing Project 1989a: *Becoming a Writer*. Walton-on-Thames: Thomas Nelson, p. 48.

Alongside these considerations of generating and organizing information, teachers and researchers have identified and studied problems children have with revision. Scardamalia and Bereiter considered children's apparent inability to revise their writing: redrafting just meant copying out neatly. Is this due, as some suggest, to egocentrism, a lack of understanding of the reader's point of view. Or is it because children 'do not have an internal feedback system that allows evaluation to become part of the writing process'. To continue in their words which capture best their approach to writing development:

In the external feedback system that regulates conversation, evaluation is triggered by signals from the conversational partner – signs of incomprehension, disbelief, boredom etc. In writing nothing happens to trigger evaluation. Furthermore if children do stop to evaluate, they have the problem of switching back to generation without having lost track of where they were in that process. In other words, there is an executive control problem. (Bereiter and Scardamalia, 1985, p. 122)

While it might be questioned whether it is true to say that 'in writing, nothing happens to trigger evaluation', a statement that seems to ignore a child's experience as a reader, the general argument provides an interesting alternative to notions of immaturity, egocentrism or lack of basic skills. Their analysis suggests that lack of revision reflects inexperience in, or lack of information about, ways of evaluating a text.

Bereiter and Scardamalia went on to look at the effect that prompt cards had on children's revisions. The cards included such evaluative statements as 'I'm getting away from the main point'/'I think this could be said more clearly'/'This is good', and directives such as 'I'd better leave this point out'/'I'd better change the wording'. They found that the prompts helped children to identify their problems. As one child said: 'you can use the cards to realize what you're saying'. But this simple feedback system did not, on its own, necessarily help children work out how to make substantial improvements to their writing.

Teachers starting from practice rather than from cognitive psychology have come to similar conclusions about the types of support children need for revision. For example, Glenda Walton in a Shropshire Middle School found that merely insti- tuting a revision stage in the children's work on a piece of writing did not provide enough support for her pupils. She suggested that children choose a partner with whom they felt able to work on improving their texts. Each pair was then given Card One (figure 5.5a). Following their discussion, a second card was given dealing with spelling, punctuation and vocabulary (figure 5.5b).

Through this and similar techniques, teachers have sup- ported the use children make of their mental processes, allowing them to extend existing language behaviours to their writing. There is a recognition that to become a skilled writer involves much more than learning about spelling and punctu- ation; the craft of writing is far more complex than that.

Pair work   **CARD ONE**

Choose a partner to work with

Your task   *Partner's task*

Read your work aloud   Listen carefully to
                                                           your partner's reading

Both of you

Try and answer the following questions:
1. Do you think the writing is interesting/enjoyable?
2. Is there anything missing in this piece?
3. Is there anything which is not clear or accurate?
4. Can you suggest any helpful words or expressions?
5. Can you suggest a more suitable beginning or ending to the piece?
6. Do you think it is too long or too short?
7. Can anything be missed out?
8. Has the writer written what (s)he was asked to do?
Write down suggested improvements on a separate piece of paper.

Pair work   **CARD TWO**

With your partner, read through your writing again.

Try and answer the following questions:
1. Are there any spelling mistakes? Underline them in pencil.
2. Check the punctuation. Are the full stops and capital letters in the
   right places? Correct them in pencil.
3. Show, on your writing, where you wish to make alterations.
4. Ask the teacher at this point if you feel you need more help.
5. Write out your revised version.

Figure 5.5   *Cards one (a) and two (b) for paired work at the revision
stage.*
Source: National Writing Project 1990d: *Responding to and Assessing Writing.*
Walton-on-Thames: Thomas Nelson, p. 36.

6

Writing with and for Others

The 'process' approach to the teaching of writing brought about many significant changes. The pupil's role changed from novitiate to author, and the teacher's role changed from giver of rules to demonstrator of a craft. New classroom strategies still made room for writing as a means of personal expression and exploration. But, in addition, there developed a focus on the mental behaviour of the child-as-writer. A child's problems with writing were seen as a natural consequence of an inexperienced person coping with new cognitive demands. The teacher's task was to develop an environment that would foster and support the child's gradual control of the writing process.

There was another shift. This was the recognition of the child as responsible for decisions about writing: about when to write and what to write; about which piece of draft writing should be developed into a final form; about what changes should be made to drafts, and about how it should be laid out, illustrated and published. New status was conferred on the child who was seen as being in control of her or his writing and as an owner of the writing process. Donald Graves explains his view of the young writer's role in his comparison of renters and owners:

Most writers rent their pieces and the teachers own them. Renters speak differently from owners: renters say 'Let him fix it – I pay the rent'; owners say, 'In the Spring we're gonna reseed the lawn, in the fall we're going to put in a new partition here with an opening between the kitchen and the dining room'. Now what happens is that the owners – and the ownership occurs at the point of the information – get very fussy about the appearance of the place. So in reality the surface features are helped more by ownership than by renting. (Graves, 1981, p. 7)

The ownership metaphor has become a central one in many process-based writing curricula. It is a term which brings with it another major thrust in the argument about writing development: that of ensuring that what is owned is worth while having. To be worth while a piece of writing needs to be seen by the children to be relevant to their lives, not just their future lives in terms of jobs and further education, but in terms of their current needs as young participants in a literacy culture. Just as adults write for specific purposes and for specific audiences – shopping lists, thank-you letters, application forms, a diary – so children need to use writing to achieve defined ends and to meet the needs of specified readers. Tasks in school need to demonstrate that writing is a purposeful social activity. It is read by someone and it is designed to achieve some outcome. Margaret Wallen, one of the National Writing Project coordinators, summed up the views of many teachers developing the writing curriculum when she wrote:

There is no doubt that learning occurs during the writing process as writers organise and recreate knowledge on the page. Surely the opportunity for learning is greatest when the learners take full responsibility for identifying the purpose of their writing, and shape and focus it themselves for a reader who really exists? . . . When children perceive that there is a readership for their writing beyond that offered by the teacher, their motivation and enthusiasm increase enormously. This gives the impetus to sustain effort through several drafts and gives the teacher an unquestionable justification for demanding technical accuracy and good presentation. Children at last see the point of the old exhortation 'Take more pride in your work', for it is their work at last and not the teacher's. (NWP, 1989c, pp. 7–8)

In the light of this concern with the purpose and audience of writing, earlier 'cognitive' process approaches that concerned themselves with the writer's problems in constructing a text began to be supplemented by a 'social' approach which could introduce children to writing as a social practice.

Audiences for writing

The surveys of children's writing diet summarized earlier showed teachers that children did not often have opportunities to *use* writing. Even when teachers might think that writing was purposeful, children's perceptions did not confirm that belief. Too often pupils reported that they wrote because that was what they were asked to do and that the only audience for their writing would be the teacher. The result of this reflection was a search for curriculum approaches that would provide new audiences and purposes for children's writing.

The notions that children should write for an audience and for a purpose were not unfamiliar when they appeared in 'process' approach curricula. They have been part of the text-book recommendations for 15 to 20 years. A wealth of research, from the Schools Council Writing Research Unit (Britton et al., 1975) on, has stressed the importance of a purpose and a sense of audience for the development of children's competence as writers. The Bullock Report (DES, 1975) noted, after discussing the need for children to experience a range of contexts for writing:

11.9 There is one further feature of written communication which is no less important in the development of children's competence: the nature of the 'audience' to which the writing is addressed. The writer's sense of audience is one of the ways in which the quality of the communication can be assessed. It has long been realised, and research has confirmed the fact, that by far the largest amount of writing in schools is explicitly or implicitly directed at the teacher. The remaining small proportion is divided between writing for self and writing for other pupils. Clearly the teacher has the responsibility of providing continuity in his capacity of principal receiver of what the children write. Nevertheless, we believe that writing for other audiences should be encouraged. If a child knows that what he is writing is going to interest and entertain others, he will be more careful with its presentation. Unfortunately, large numbers of children are still denied this assurance, and their work does not emerge from the covers of the exercise book. (DES, 1975, p. 166)

But while the need to develop a 'sense of audience' was recognized, the response to the recommendations tended to be fairly piecemeal. Two factors help explain the lack of implementation of 'writing for an audience' practices in the 1970s. One was that, while providing children with an audience for their writing was considered an important classroom activity, it was viewed as separable from other activities such as learning to spell, learning to use different varieties of writing, writing expressively and so on. 'Writing for an audience' could be interpreted as just another writing skill to be learned by children rather than as a central guiding principle for all writing activities. Thus in many classrooms (mainly primary) children would write a story for younger pupils, or write a guide book for new entrants, but such activities would have little effect on the classroom organization, the contents of the stationery cupboard or the teacher's role. Compared with the activities described below, these writing tasks tended to be teacher-initiated and teacher-directed, carried out in order to satisfy the curriculum requirements of letting children write for an audience. Why and how the writing was to happen was not questioned, and the writing was rarely read and evaluated by its intended audience. In the children's minds it is unclear how far such activities were seen as different from other writing tasks. The audiences and purposes were not, in process approach terminology, 'real'.

A second factor limiting the uptake of 'writing for an audience' activities in the primary phase was the use of evidence from cognitive developmental psychology to argue that children's development as writers depended on their ability to imagine another's perspective. Younger children, some argued (e.g. Britton et al., 1975), will find writing for an absent reader difficult at first because such writing demands the ability to decentre, an ability which, according to Piagetian research, develops slowly in the early years. According to this argument, writing for different readers will develop later than the ability to talk to different audiences as in writing there is no immediate reactive receiver of the message. This hypothesis seemed to indicate that writing in the Infants' classroom should be predominantly personal or expressive with little reference to intended readership, and only later should children be encouraged to move to new 'spectator' writing roles where the reactions of others could be considered.

These two factors – lack of genuine activities to develop a sense of audience and a belief in young children's inherent egocentrism – were mutually reinforcing. Without opportunities to experience 'real' audiences, young children failed to demonstrate an ability to write for others, drifting into familiar personal narratives, the main thrust of all their other writing. Such writing, in turn, convinced teachers that activities involving writing for others should not be central to the curriculum of young children.

In the wake of the 'process' approach, the new emphases on the writer and the construction of texts (and the de-emphasis on the text and the child's production skills) led to a re-emergence and re-evaluation of activities to write for different audiences and purposes. The approaches that developed demonstrated how activities could be much more than mere curriculum add-ons. Furthermore, the work that young children produced when audiences were 'real' threw into doubt notions of young children's egocentrism (at the same time, psychological research findings questioned many of Piagetian conclusions about egocentric thought, c.g. Donaldson, 1978). Margaret Wallen summarizes the way that teachers began to view 'writing for an audience' activities:

Writing for new audiences carries with it important implications for all writing done in schools. Audience cannot be viewed as an isolated variable. In the past, many teachers have experimented with, for example, writing stories for younger children, but in order fully to exploit the potential for deepening understanding of the writing process which such experiences offer, it is necessary to rethink other aspects of the writing context. (NWP, 1989c, p. 9)

Some edited accounts from National Writing Project case studies provide examples of the ways in which children develop as writers once audiences and purposes are found (see NWP, 1989c for fuller descriptions).

Minnie Anderson, a reception teacher in a Newcastle school, was concerned about how to provide four and five-year-olds with opportunities to write for real audiences when their writing was still at a stage where it often needed to be read aloud in order to be understood. She writes:

Should we resolve this dilemma by withholding real but absent audiences until later, or should we as adults scribe their voiced thoughts for them?

Baking cakes became the catalyst for a writing activity that would help answer such questions. The activity began with shopping for the ingredients. Children visited the local supermarket armed with their 'lists' – sheets of card upon which labels identifying every ingredient were firmly stuck. The children matched the labels to those of goods on the shelves, and finally made their purchases.

The cakes were duly made, with plenty left over to send to children in the nursery class. Having dispatched the cakes with a signed card, the reception children eagerly awaited the response. Back it came in the form of a large 'thank-you for the cakes' letter signed by the nursery children, with a request for the recipe. Excellent. They now had a real audience and a real purpose for writing. But there was also a problem: how does one write a recipe for an audience of non-readers? The reception children were discovering at first hand that the demands of a real audience can be quite taxing for a writer. The solution for this class lay within their own experience and, after lengthy deliberation, they set about constructing a recipe.

The children adapted their stuck-on shopping list method and produced a sequenced recipe with packaging to show each ingredient – including the eggshells. Precise pictures of spoons showing quantities were carefully included within the 'method' part of the recipe. The finished pictogram recipe, with certain key words and phrases scribed by the teacher, stretched across the width of the classroom. On completion, four children carefully delivered the recipe, winding their way through the school corridors and halls until they reached the nursery.

The nursery audience 'read' the recipe and successfully baked their own cakes. Their only problem concerned the quantity of eggs required – was it three or six? It all depended on how you read the eggshells!

Through this collaborative venture both classes found a form of writing to each other that was suited to their own expertise and carefully tailored to suit the needs of their particular audience.

News of the recipe had by then spread throughout the school, and the reception class could observe what happens if your audience changes and your writing has to accommodate a different range of writing experiences and expectations. A number of eleven year olds were invited to borrow the cake recipe. They read, they cooked and they evaluated for themselves! In answer to the question 'Was it easy to follow?' there were responses like: 'We measured the flour wrongly and put too much fat in. The first time they were very greasy. The second time they were nice'. These reactions helped to highlight for the young writers the different expectations of a more mature group of readers – perhaps they had skimmed the recipe too quickly or made hasty assumptions.

The recipe was then rewritten by the eleven year olds, for someone of their own age. The new versions were displayed with the original so that the reception class authors could compare the contrasting styles, and recognise the needs of an older audience. (NWP 1989a, p. 36–7)

This account demonstrates just what very early writers are capable of achieving in writing when classroom conditions are structured in certain ways. Infants can produce excellent writing, without signs of egocentrism, that serve their purposes and audience well. Another example of young writers' achievements comes from a Dudley school where 60 children in two reception classes decided to produce guides to their school for four and five-year-olds that could be left as colouring books by the home liaison teacher. The teachers, Marilyn Short and Linda Stringer, wrote of the children's competence thus:

We wanted the book to use the pupil's own words so that they should know they were responsible for the finished product. In fact, their writing showed such an insight into the crucial concerns of five-year-olds that it would have been both impossible and inappropriate for us to impose our ideas. (NWP, 1989c, p. 33) (figure 6.1)

Figure 6.1   *Bromley the Bear from a reception class school guide for four to five-year-olds.*
Source: National Writing Project 1989c: *Audiences for Writing*. Walton-on-Thames: Thomas Nelson, p. 34.

Similarly, there's the example of a class of six-year-olds in Vivienne Miller's Dorset class who had written stories for younger children. These were edited, illustrated and bound. Finally, after looking at published books in the library, each child added an autobiographical sketch on the back such as that shown in figure 6.2. When all 27 had been written, the teacher noticed that every child had, without explicit instruction, used the third person to talk about themselves. Theories about egocentric writers are forcefully challenged by such evidence.

The achievements of the young writers in these and many comparable examples raise a serious challenge to models of child development that plot acquisition as a series of stages, with certain writing varieties and functions preceding others.

Figure 6.2 *Helen Gilber's autobiographical sketch.*
Source: National Writing Project 1989c: *Audiences for Writing*. Walton-on-
Thames: Thomas Nelson, p. 22.

Examples of practice show what children can do when provided with a rich writing environment, and place in doubt
any account of writing that shows growth as linear. The strong
evidence from the National Writing Project experiences is that
children can tackle practically any writing task from the very
early years as long as they understand what it is about and
who it is for. As they gain more experience, so they will be
able to refine their competence in different varieties of writing.
As the DES National Curriculum document *English for Ages 5
to 16* (1989) states 'language development is not linear but
recursive' (para. 15.20).

Another notable feature, related to the children's demon-
stration of their ability to adapt their written language for

different audiences, is the increased pride children have in their work once they know where it is going and why. Writing techniques which used to be in the form of exhortations 'make a plan before you start'/'check your work carefully'/'now write it up neatly' become accepted by the children as useful and necessary aids to their texts' development. Drafting is recognized by the children as the way 'to get it right' before it is made public. Editing is initiated by the children as often as by the teacher when they realize that their writing will become part of the Infants' library or will go on sale in the local newsagents. Children are often ready to articulate their feelings towards their work. For instance, top Juniors in a Birmingham school, who had been preparing a 'Guide to Hinduism', reflected on the need to use each other to help revise drafts and on the need to get it right:

If [our friends] think it's bad we can change a little bit – we can change it and get it right. If they find some mistakes we could change it again, get more information.
We checked rough copies for spellings and we checked to see if we had wrong information.
It's going to other places and other people are going to read it.
(Ann Davis and Barbara Grayson, NWP, 1989c, p. 51)

The quality of the product also matters: the paper, the handwriting, the typing, the layout and so on all become issues for the children. In example after example, teachers have found that the writer's behaviour changes when texts no longer reside in exercise books, but meet communicative needs; when they are initiated and controlled by the pupil and when children are provided with the materials appropriate to the writer's function.

Writing as a joint venture

Whether the children are writing recipes for their cakes, books for younger children or guides to their school or to their religion, a striking characteristic of the work is its collaborative nature. Children writing in such classrooms see writing not as an isolated task, a strictly personal affair between paper and self, but as a joint venture in which other children and adults can provide ideas, support and advice. Writing becomes for these children a social activity in which they have to learn ways of interacting effectively. For example, children are introduced to ways of providing comments on drafts, learning about others' sensitivities to criticism. An advice sheet on responding to writing put together by pupils from a Somerset Middle School included the following thoughts:

First you remember that whatever you think of somebody else's work they may have spent a long time on it. What you think is drivel may be the result of hard work and a lot of thought. The last thing they want or need is you being rude about it. (NWP, 1990a, p. 35)

Teachers, too, have become more sensitive to the effects of criticism, partly from becoming writers themselves and reflecting on their own reactions to comments, and partly from the realization that once writing is *for* someone else, then their comments need to be put alongside those of the intended audience. The teacher is no longer the sole arbiter of text quality but one of a number of different respondents. A noticeable change that occurs when there are respondents other than the teacher is that children become more reflective about their work. Children often take for granted that teachers will be critical and want improvement, but when peers or outsiders are critical, conflicts can emerge in the child's mind that need to be thought about and acted upon.

An example from Sue Cannell's fourth-year Junior class in a Shropshire school illustrates this well. Rebecca, a ten-year-old, had, along with the rest of her class, been writing a story for the Infants. She planned, drafted and showed her work to her 'response partner', then tried out the draft with the intended audience before revising it completely. She reflected on her reactions to the comments in an interview with Ned Ratcliffe, the Shropshire Project coordinator.

Rebecca did not take kindly to suggestions from her partner about how her story might be improved and she ignored them: 'I didn't like it at first. I took no notice at first.' She volunteered, though, when there was an opportunity to give a trial reading of her story to a group of Infants. Their response was not as she had anticipated. 'They didn't like it. They said, "Mmmm . . . a bit short . . . Not enough interesting words . . . Make it longer." And they wanted a bit of make believe in it. It was very embarrassing. I felt . . . hmmm . . . if they don't like that, I'm not doing any more. Then I thought, everybody's writing much better stories. I'm going to try . . . so I made an effort.'

After this experience with the Infants, she took more notice of her partner but she still didn't change anything if she felt the original was all right . . . 'Some things my partner said, I disagreed with.' ('What did you do, then, if there's something your partner says and you disagree?') 'Well, you sometimes look at it from different angles, but it doesn't always work. You still keep arguing. But if it's your story you put it how you think best, but don't completely forget the comments'. (NWP, 1990a, p. 66)

Rebecca's remark that it was *her* story brings out the central principle that guided the teacher's behaviour during the writing activity. The teacher provided support for Rebecca's writing through discussions about Infant reading materials and through setting up meetings between writers and their audience. But once the support structures were in place, Rebecca was left responsible for deciding what to write, how to revise and when she had reached the final draft. Once the writing is seen to be owned by the child then former notions of the teacher being the 'principal receiver of what the children write' (Bullock Report, para. 11.9 quoted above) and all that such a role implies come under question. A shift in the location of power from teacher to child takes place; a shift, as will be discussed in the next chapter, that has brought with it some dilemmas for the teacher.

The new 'process' approach to writing also brought with it a shift in the location of the writing events. When the teacher is in control of what is written, and when texts are confined to exercise books, then the writing task is contained within the classroom. But when purposes for writing extend far beyond those of practising skills, and audiences reach beyond the school, then it follows that children are no longer going to be writing at their desks. Instead, children will be found writing with and for Senior Citizens in the local community centre; exchanging stories and journals with children at other ends of the country; inviting members of the community in to school to be interviewed for the school newspaper; or talking with their relatives before writing up biographies or local histories which would later be sold in the community. School might be where most of the actual writing takes place, but informants and ideas come as often as not from outside. The finished product often ends up in the local newsagent or in a local resident's home, far places from the exercise book or wall display. Furthermore, the end products are not always written. Other media such as radio, film and plays often result from the original work theme, as children consider what the most effective outcomes of their work might be. Former divisions between reading, writing and talk begin to break down, as activities become language events to achieve specific and immediate ends rather than skill acquisition exercises in preparation for the future.

Importantly, too, the location of the language events is not confined to English or Language curriculum slots. Many subject teachers were quick to recognize how writing could be exploited in their area as something more than a means of recording what had happened in the lesson. One example from an Avon Home Economics class helps to illustrate this point.

The class was making Easter nests when some of the children noticed that the packets of Cadbury's mini-eggs varied in quantity. They researched all the packets and then decided to write to complain. The first draft of their letter to Cadbury's is shown in figure 6.3. After working on this draft as a group, electing a neat handwriter and so on, they produced a final draft (figure 6.4). The finished letter has interesting amendments. There is an improvement in spelling and handwriting but, more interestingly, there are choices of style which show a recognition of appropriate style for a friendly but complaining letter. Compare, for instance, their signatures and their post-

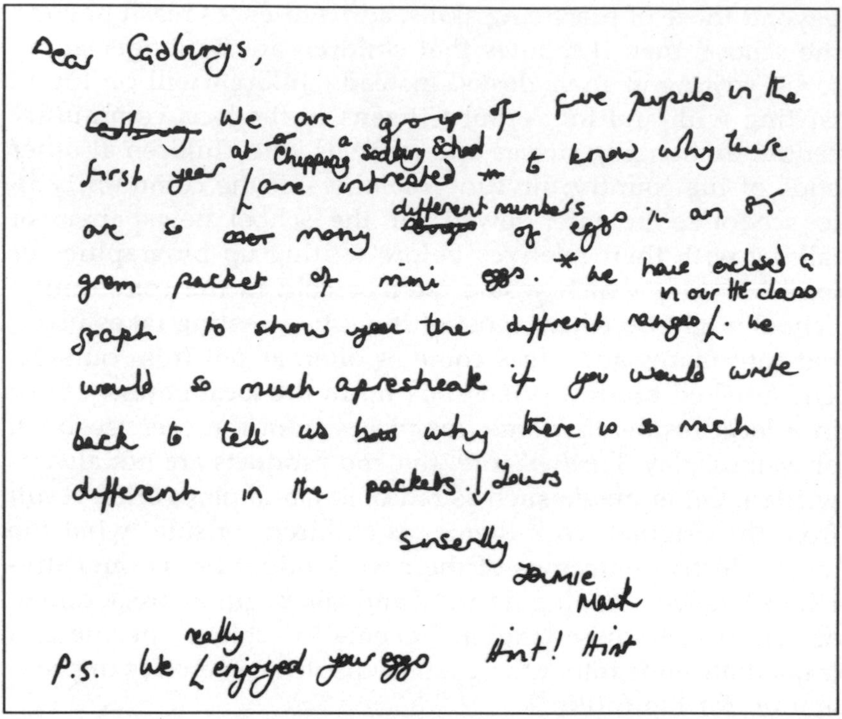

Figure 6.3   *Original draft of letter of complaint to Cadbury's.*
Source: National Writing Project 1990f: *Ways of Looking*. Walton-on-Thames:
Thomas Nelson, p. 11.

script. Incidentally, Cadbury's did reply (quoted by Czerniewska, in NWP, 1990f, p. 12). What is clear from this example is
that the Home Economics teacher recognized her role as a
teacher of writing and allowed the children to build on their
observations and to use the information for a purposeful end.

It is hard to convey in just a few pages the excitement, even
euphoria, that teachers express when they recount the writing
activities that the children have engaged in. The writing curriculum has not only been revised but revitalized. The sense
of optimism shared by all involved about the consequences
of their innovations is perhaps best summed up in a further
extract from Margaret Wallen's article:

No longer are [children] writing to tell the teacher something the
teacher already knows, or simply because the teacher tells them to.
If the situation is real, their writing has authority. They have some-

> Dear Cadburys,
> We are a group of five pupils in the 1st year at Chipping Sodbury School who are intrested to know why there are so many diffrent numbers of eggs in an 85g packet of mini eggs. We are using your eggs in our H.E Lesson to decorate our choclate nests. We have enclosed a graph to show you the diffrent ranges in our H.E class. We would so much apriciate if you would write back to tell us why there is so much diffronce in the packets
>
> Yours
> Sincerly
>
> Becky Sweet, Jamie Collard, Mark JENNINGS, Mabel Shaw, Anthony Patterson.
>
> P.S. We really enjoyed your eggs.

Figure 6.4 *Final version to letter to Cadbury's showing interesting amendments.*
Source: National Writing Project 1990f: *Ways of Looking*. Walton-on-Thames: Thomas Nelson, p. 12.

thing to say to the world at large and they no longer need someone else to tell them how to say it. They have become more independent, no longer inferior partners in the reader/writer relationship. They have learned that, in the real world, writing is about power. (NWP, 1989c, p. 9)

7

What are they Writing About?

Anyone who observes or participates in a classroom where a 'process' approach to writing is being put into practice will pick up the enthusiasm of teachers and children towards the writing tasks. Scattered around will be plenty of decorated and laminated books written by children for other children. Any adult who stops near a display of these will soon be surrounded by the authors wishing to show you their books and happy to explain the drafts they went through, the discussions they had with the potential readership and their plans for sequels. There will probably be a designated writing corner, fully equipped with typewriter, writing paper and implements of all kinds, perhaps a word processor. Writing on the walls, from labels to lists to mounted texts, will capture the spirit of the children's involvement in their own writing. A chat with any of the groups writing will demonstrate how much the children know about editing practices, with words like final draft and proofreading rolling easily off even the youngest tongues. Above all, it will be a classroom full of talk and activity as the children collaborate in every aspect of the writing process.

It is not hard for even the casual visitor to be persuaded that you can give pupils more control over the writing process by enhancing the writing curriculum so that topics are pupil-led, audiences and purposes are real, and that skills of spelling and handwriting are developed through editing of their own work. Even the most die-hard supporter of 'teaching basics' would admit that the 'process-based' writing environment leads to more committed and confident young writers than did any teacher-led, exercise-based approaches where children write in isolation for undefined readers and purposes.

The 'process' orientation has re-focused the curriculum on the functions that writing serves and on the writer's behaviour during the production of a text. Major claims have been made about the success of the new approach in terms of children's writing development. There are also important challenges to the theory and the practice. One line of criticism questions the extent that the new curriculum has concerned itself with what children write about. Related questions are raised about the extent to which school experiences of the writing process adequately prepare children for the writing they will use in later life. While proponents of the process approach claim that their curriculum empowers children, critics argue whether the 'power' has any reality in terms of children's prospects in the world outside school. Do the choices and opportunities about what to write when and to whom allow children to go beyond culturally expected behaviour? The ascriptions of power and choice to those pupils who experience a 'process' approach need to be scrutinized as they may disguise the fact that we have done nothing to challenge existing social attitudes, prejudices and divisions. Janet White raises the issue thus:

Giving pupils power over the writing process does not necessarily mean that they are writing more powerful texts . . . [perhaps] all we have helped pupils to own are versions of cultural cliches. (NWP, 1990d, p. 58)

White and others have looked specifically at the writing of boys and girls to see the extent to which changes in the writing curriculum have in fact changed children's experiences, have empowered them in some new way. The questions raised make us look again at what it means to say we are creating a successful writing environment. Perhaps, on closer inspection, the involved, committed, animated young writers we see in the classroom may delude us into thinking that we have changed children's futures in some way. To quote from one of White's evaluative papers on the work of the National Writing Project:

Effective teaching may very well betray us into an idealistic optimism which glosses the problem of locating centres of power in writing. We can't leap from the reality of a successful classroom into the reality of the outside world any more than we can assume that young writers fledged in the more enabling conditions of a National Writing Project classroom will magically soar above the many problematic aspects that still surround writing in the world at large. (White, 1986, p. 3)

The critical point being raised concerns the social nature of literacy. There is a strong risk that the enthusiastic adoption of 'process' approaches has obscured or left unquestioned differences between language use among different classes, genders and ethnic groups. Concepts such as 'audience' and 'purpose' may have become unproblematic variables in the learning equation, disguising the fact that there are strong cultural norms about who can write in particular ways to particular people. Furthermore the apparent 'power' given to pupils to determine what they write about can lead to a neglect of the actual *content* of writing and can play down the conflicts inherent in acts of writing (Faigley, 1986).

An example from Pam Gilbert's study of writing and gender illustrates this argument (Gilbert, 1988). She challenges the view that the curriculum is successful as long as children want to write and are found to be writing with enthusiasm. Such a view, she argues, leaves the content of children's writing unchallenged and unchallengeable, thus allowing culturally embedded ideologies to pass almost unnoticed. To demonstrate her point she tells of an Australian class of nine to ten-year-olds whose teacher was trying to implement a writing workshop environment. The children were encouraged to write and 'publish' books for other young readers on topics of their choice. They worked collaboratively in self-chosen groups and, in all ways possible, were encouraged to act as writers.

One group of four boys began constructing a story called 'Bloodbath Efa Bunnies' – an 'efa bunny' was a lisping Easter Bunny, the in-vogue character of jokes. The boys' story entailed a violent attack from the efa bunnies, with the four boys, plus another, warding them off with various deadly weapons. 'Anzac comradeship and Rambo individualism are intertwined as the boys cover their mates, shoot moonbeam lasers that rebound with deadly accuracy, and eventually "save the world".' But it was more than just a violent boys' war story as it also featured the girls in their class and revealed the male writers' stereotyped views and their knowledge and acceptance of a gendered ideology. Most of the girls, all given their real names, had predictable parts in the story, for example, having relationships with the boys and saying 'I love you', and were either killed or married off. One girl shared a different fate. She was the biggest in the class and jumped on the marauding bunnies. The boys' text reads: '"AAAAA! My God! Super Blubber!" they said as they got up. "Run!".' As Gilbert says, 'No need to kill off this female: her size and aggression have effectively excluded her anyway. (What worse fate for a girl than to be called Super Blubber?)' Two female class members had no role in the story; one was a new girl, and the other a quiet Asian girl.

In line with practice common in many schools, the story was typed, bound and added to the school library. Thus, without any criticism or questioning of its content, the boys' tale was validated as a class book. At a time when teachers are more and more aware of the need to check school resources for instances of sexism and racism, children's own-produced materials are apparently being admitted into the class stock unchecked. (Interestingly, Gilbert discovered that this particular book disappeared from the library two days later.)

This one, not untypical, classroom incident raises a whole set of questions about approaches to writing that attribute great powers to the individual writer but that fail to acknowledge literacy as a socially constructed practice or set of practices. In an effort to ensure that children are given 'freedom' to write as they want for others or for themselves, questions are ignored about the cultural origins of the individual writer's goals. The 'process' approach, as has been described above, emphasizes qualities of originality, spontaneity and creativity. The approach builds on earlier notions of 'personal growth', of children discovering their own means of self-expression, of exploring their own feelings and personal experiences. But it overcomes some of the problems of teachers feeling reticent or unable to support children while they create their texts. Whereas in the 1960s, teachers were wary of interfering with the child's 'natural' development, the move in the late 1970s and 1980s towards a more 'cognitive' approach to the process of writing allowed more intervention in the writer's behaviour. Children can be taught ways of organizing information and revising texts. The creation of a text is recognized as hard as well as exhilarating, as prone to failure as well as to success. However, within 'process' doctrine, there still remains a firm emphasis on the notion of the writer as an originator of her or his meaning. Terms such as 'children as authors' and 'children as owners of the writing process' carry an underlying message that as long as teachers provide an environment in which personal experiences are valued and where a published author's techniques can be practised, then children will be enabled to express themselves effectively in writing.

Conceiving of the student as an 'author' gives to the student writer the mythical status of original meaning-maker, places value and primacy on the student's first-hand, personal experiences, and valorises the student text as authentic human experience. Student's texts are seen to be so closely aligned to the individual child and that child's original making of meaning, that they are 'beyond criticism'. (Gilbert, 1988)

To question the content of children's writing is not an easy step to take. It seems to conflict with deeply held views about valuing what children do, about allowing them choice and about starting from where they are; views about individualism, discovery and self-expression which are at the core of post-Plowden primary education. Critical evaluation of children's personal choice of topics involves a shift in thinking about children and education towards recognizing learning as a social interactive process and seeing literacy as a social practice in which children are differently positioned according to their sex and ethnic background. 'The child-centred ideology needs to be replaced with one that emphasises the socio-cultural and discursive bases of knowledge and learning' (Edwards and Mercer, 1987, p. 168).

Observing what boys and girls write

A few examples from teachers who have begun exploring issues of gender and writing in their classrooms demonstrate the type of shift entailed.

An opportunity to study the behaviour of girls and boys on a specific writing task arose in a Bedfordshire class of nine to ten-year-olds (NWP, 1990d, p. 20–6). The children had been listening to a school radio series 'The Odyssey' and after each episode were invited by their teacher, Norah Arnold, to write about any part of the story they liked. Eventually, the stories formed a wall display which was later taken down and compiled into a book. It was only at this point that the teacher began to take a close look at what different children had chosen to write about and to recognize that the choice of subject matter and orientation to the subject fell along gendered lines. She categorized the writing into three types:

affective   – pertaining to affections or emotions;
power   – concerning authority, control or personal ascendancy;
violence   – concerning physical force or bloodthirstiness.

Analysis of the topics that the children had chosen to write about or illustrate showed that girls' writing was far more likely to fall under the 'affective' category, while boys' writing was predominantly centred around 'power' and 'violence'. Norah Arnold writes about her analysis:

The more I looked at the material, the more instances I found where girls had written about the same happenings as those chosen by the boys, but the girls had accentuated the feelings of the people involved, whereas the boys had been more concerned with sheer violence or power. When writing about Odysseus forcing Circe to return his men to human form after she had turned them into swine, one girl ended up writing, 'Circe asked Odysseus to stay with her but Odysseus told her that he had to get back to his wife'. Another girl wrote, 'Circe said to Odysseus "stay with me and be my love".' On the other hand, writing about the same happening, the boys emphasised the power and strength of Odysseus and wrote such things as: 'Then suddenly Odysseus raised his sword. "Don't kill me" cried Circe. "Who are you really?" "I am Odysseus, the sacker of cities. Set my men free".' . . .

Attitudes to Odysseus' adventures in the Underworld were markedly different between boys and girls. The girls tended to change the ghosts into friendly creatures who made remarks such as "Hello. Welcome to the underworld." They stressed the comforting nature of Odysseus' leadership and the fact that his men trusted him. Several boys, on the other hand, were fascinated by Odysseus' sacrifice of the goat, the trench of blood and the attempts of the ghosts to drink it. Only one girl mentioned the sacrifice and the blood and then only briefly in a matter of fact way in order to explain the next point she was going to make. The boys' drawings of the ghosts in the Underworld almost invariably had swords sticking from some part of their ghostly anatomy, an aspect not mentioned in the dramatisation at all.

A similar comparison of boys' and girls' writing choices was made by two Dudley sixth-formers, Peter Howe and Andrea Smallwood (NWP, 1990d, p. 26–7). They looked at the writing of six and seven-year-olds who had written stories for younger children. They talked to the children about their stories and then analysed the content. In their account, they commented on the high standard of presentation, and the immense enjoyment all children had had in writing the books. But what stood out for them was the difference in content. A short extract gives the flavour of their findings:

There were two main categories: fairytales and gangs or groups. The most remarkable feature was that without exception girls chose one type of story whilst boys chose another. In fact, it would be quite possible to identify the sex of every writer merely on the content. Typical titles by the girls were 'The Pretty Princess', 'The Mermaid', 'The Book of Fairyland' and 'The Princess Party'. Boys write stories with titles such as 'The Gang' and 'The Dustbin Family'. The substance of most stories by girls tended to be marriage, birthday parties and beautiful princesses and all the stories had happy end-ings. Races, fights, spiders, darkness, cricket and cars constituted the majority of the boys' work. Boys wrote far more aggressive stories. Frequently, one character achieved power over another. The girls placed their heroines passively subordinate to other characters.

Free writing?

Monitoring what children write has caused teachers to question exactly what is meant by 'free writing choice'. Can school tasks be isolated and freed from the constraints imposed by the inequalities of the outside world? The answer is that they cannot. In the classroom as much as in the playground, home and workplace, girls and boys are running different races. Differences in the choices of what to write about revealed in the accounts above are part of a complex process in which children are learning about culturally defined behaviours. Girls and boys not only write about different things, they also prefer different writing forms, girls showing a strong preference for narrative, boys choosing more fact-based forms. Girls overall do better than boys in language-related subjects as reflected in examination results at all levels, and more girls select language subjects for study in secondary schools, while boys predominate in the science-based curriculum strands. These choices are well known and often seem to make the educational process somehow equable: girls perform well in some things; boys in others. But what is rarely asked is why girls' excellence in language, and specifically their higher writing competence, is not reflected in their later job positions.

We need to ask why it is that thousands of able girl writers leave school and go into secretarial jobs, in the course of which they will patiently revise the semi-literate manuscripts of their male bosses, or else return in droves to the primary classroom, there to supervise the production of another generation of pen-wise girls. (White, 1985, p. 2)

Girls do get jobs in other literacy-related careers, but it is men who get the top positions in journalism, advertising, academia and publishing. Women are there but 'a degree of invisibility surrounds their roles; customarily those of researchers, assistants and ubiquitous typists/secretaries' (White, 1986, p. 8). Women also become writers but few get listed among the 'greats', and few get studied for public examinations or get extracted for textbook exercises. Thus there seems to be a subtle reinforcement process in operation by which girls become good at writing but fail to see themselves as participants in high-level writing careers. Their lowered aspirations can be seen, too, in their attitudes towards the subject they excel in – language. In an Assessment of Performance Unit survey 200 15-year-olds were asked whether they thought it was a good thing or not 'that more girls obtain qualifications in languages and more boys obtain qualifications in scientific subjects'. About a third of both boys and girls agreed that it was a good thing with statements such as: 'Girls are less able to take the academic subjects. This is to do with their home and life styles' (girl). 'Most girls end up as secretaries etc., and boys as engineers etc.' (girl). 'It is a good thing that boys get science qualifications as a fair percentage will need it for jobs, but girls don't need language qualifications as they will be at home with children' (boy). Only about a quarter of the girls (14 per cent of boys) thought that there should be less stereotyping in subject choices with statements such as: 'Girls may find sciences boring and keep away and so never know if they could succeed – same with boys and English' (unpublished research from 1983 DES Secondary Language Survey, quoted in White, 1986, p. 18).

By looking at girls' and boys' choices in writing against this broader cultural backcloth, more searching questions can be asked about the implementation of a writing process approach. One can ask, for instance, how the range of purposes and audiences being promoted might be challenging or fostering particular attitudes and abilities. Is the popularity of writing stories for younger children likely to provide equal experiences for boys and girls? Will it be new for boys but just more of the familiar practice of narrative writing for girls? Will it be used by boys simply as an opportunity for rehearsing stories of fantasy and violence? Do writing tasks which encourage collaborative composition and editing lead to new experiences in unfamiliar roles? Do boys dominate the talk while girls take over the fine editing, reinforcing accepted gendered behaviour? And behind all these questions lies a harder one about the role of the teacher as critical reader and as interrogator of prevailing social practices.

A great risk that is run in the process-based writing classroom is that the teacher as enabler and facilitator encourages, by default, uncritical acceptance of stereotyped behaviour. When the audience for a piece of writing lies outside the classroom and is a real person, be it a five-year-old sibling or an unknown adult, this should not exclude the teacher as a critical reader of the text, showing children through their reading of their own and others' writing how to interrogate texts. Two examples which show teachers exploring with children the assumptions about boys and girls in texts suggest ways of helping children recognize the socially mediated nature of all educational practices.

One example, from Rochdale, involved the teacher, Jan Smith, reading *The Turbulent Term of Tyke Tyler* to her class of eight and nine-year-olds. Three-quarters of the way through, she asked the children to draw a picture of Tyke and to guess what Tyke's real name might be. 'The disclosure at the end of the book of Tyke's identity as a girl resulted in a mixed reaction – from disbelief to outrage. Every child had believed Tyke to be a boy.' Following this, Jan Smith got the children to discuss why they thought Tyke was a boy and then to talk and write about their perceptions of gender roles. This, in turn, led to the class looking at the depiction of girls and boys in books, comics, advertisements and so on, and resulted in some letters being sent to publishers complaining about role stereotypes. They read *The Practical Princess* (in which role portrayal is far from traditional) and presented it as a puppet play in their School Book Week. The effects were evident:

Shortly after Book Week, I asked the children to begin a story remembering all the things we had talked about over the past few weeks, but giving no further direction over content, style or message.

Noticeably fewer children wrote totally single sex stories, nor did content or likely reader interest seem as closely tied to the sex of the writer as was usual for these children. (NWP, 1990d, p. 33)

A second example comes from a Dorset school where Barbara Tilbrook and Denise Wardle had been working with a class of nine and ten-year-olds on toys and gender. This topic emerged from a 'show and tell' session during which one boy announced that he did not like looking at girls' toys. The subject developed into a survey of toys owned and the discovery of considerable overlap in toy preferences. At this point an article appeared in the free press appealing for Christmas toys, and asking that they be marked for a boy or girl. This provoked much discussion and resulted in the children writing to the editor. In response, the paper sent a reporter to the class to prepare a centre-page spread on the children's views.

The reporter deliberately challenged the children and tried to provoke them, with particular reference to the boys' fondness for cuddly toys. The boys defended themselves strongly and also objected to a suggested pose for a photograph which would have shown them with fists raised at each other. . . . [When the report was published] the children were able to identify subtle differences. I, for instance, had pointed out that boys usually spoke more in discussion; this had been interpreted as: 'But she admitted that the boys are usually more assertive in class than the girls.' (NWP, 1990d, pp. 40–1)

In both these examples, the class activities went far beyond being simply writing tasks. They involved reading, role play and discussion as much as writing. What they achieved, in small but significant ways, was to show children the cultural meanings that are embodied in everyday texts such as newspapers, stories and advertisements. The children developed a heightened awareness of the responsibilities of being a writer that go far beyond understanding the composing and editing processes.

This chapter has focused on issues of gender and writing, and used them as a vehicle to question assumptions underlying certain approaches to writing development. Comparable issues about ethnicity and writing are described and discussed in NWP, 1990c. The view of literacy being fostered in these examples is one in which the individual writer is seen to be a part of the culture and in which, to paraphrase Vygotsky (1978), a child acquires not only the words of language but the intentions carried by those words and the situations implied by them.

8

Different Types of Writing

The conclusion reached in the last chapter is that the teaching of writing involves more than providing a supportive context and reflecting on the writing process. To understand writing development, we need to know not only about the writer's behaviour and the cognitive abilities of learners but also about the social interactive processes by which children and teachers construct literacy. Children do not learn to write through some form of spontaneous creative force; they learn what their culture and their school have constructed for them to learn.

The types of classrooms that have been described in the preceding chapters have tried, as their central aims, to help children see the opportunities that written varieties of language can provide and to help them understand what it is to be a writer. Some approaches are open to the criticism that the content of children's writing has been ignored or been placed above critical comment. Classroom practices have sometimes artificially isolated the writing process from its culture, ignoring how it works in society, pretending that everyone has as much right to publish or that all writing is equally valued.

These criticisms reveal a dilemma of child-centred ideology that has dominated primary education for the past 30 or so years. In writing, as in the teaching of all subjects, the direction of curriculum change has been towards 'discovery' and away from 'transmission'. Beneath a label of 'discovery' lies a view of the individual child as an active learner who relates new knowledge to past experiences, formulating and refining hypotheses and moving slowly towards the adult model. Such a view is in opposition to the 'empty vessel' image of the child who learns by absorption of new material provided by the adult instructor. 'Discovery' implies an individual search for meaning, guided and facilitated by the teacher and nurtured by a stimulating classroom environment which builds on the unique and personal experiences of each child.

But a close examination of 'discovery' methods (e.g. Edwards and Mercer, 1987) suggests that classroom contexts have been created in which pupils do not, in fact, do very much in the way of constructing their own learning. Instead, they often engage in elaborate guessing games in an attempt to find out what it is they are meant to be learning. Rather than draw on their own personal experiences, the (unintended) curriculum asks them to find out what experiences the teacher has in mind for them. An example of a guessing-game under the guise of 'discovery' is the attempt in Maths to make problems close to children's lives by talking about 'real' events. However, most children work out early on that such real-life problems are dressed-up versions of arithmetic exercises, to be solved by well-tried formulae such as 'find the smaller number and take it away from the bigger one' or 'divide the bigger number by the smaller one, and if that doesn't work, multiply'. Transmission comes disguised as discovery.

When looking at the writing classroom, questions can be asked about the hidden curriculum that guides the forms of writing that children develop and explore. Some argue that classroom processes result in children discovering only a limited set of written varieties or *genres*. Criticisms of the way in which the writing curriculum constrains children's writing development come most forcefully from proponents of the 'genre' school. They have described how children's writing is channelled towards very specific forms of writing, and they have challenged the values placed on particular genres (for example, narrative).

A description of Martin and Rothery's work (Martin, 1984; Rothery, 1984) should help to develop the 'genre' school argument. They looked at the types of writing that prevailed in Australian primary classrooms in order to discover whether certain types were more prevalent than others among particular age groups; whether there was some ordered development of types of writing and whether some forms of writing were being more highly valued than others. By examining the different types of texts that they found, they hoped to construct a typology of children's written genres. (A 'genre' is defined as 'purposeful, staged cultural activity in which human beings engage': Christie, 1984, p. 20. Below, there is a detailed discussion of the nature of genre and how knowledge of genres can inform practice.)

Martin and Rothery looked at classrooms where a process approach was operating and asked 'what do children write?' They found that certain forms of writing dominated the early years of schooling in Australia (and see Maclure, 1986, discussed in chapter 4, for a parallel example from British schools). They found that there was a fairly predictable order in which different forms of writing appeared in the Infant years. This order, they argue, does not simply reflect the linguistic complexity of particular texts, but relates to the social context of classrooms in which certain forms of writing are more highly valued than others.

The first type of writing that they found children engage in was 'labelling'. Typically, this consists of a picture plus a caption, for example, 'This is a red car.' Why is it that so many children produce such similar first texts? Martin (1984) comments:

Children are not learning to write in a vacuum, pouring out thoughts from within. Rather they are sensitively exploring their classroom environment, searching for what is required, no matter how implicit or hidden what they need to know might be. Like all successful language learners children are good sleuths. The labelling genre satisfies teachers as a first step. (Martin, 1984, p. 2)

The labelling genre develops, they argue, into the 'observation/comment' genre, the form of writing most prevalent in the first two years of primary school. Typical examples are 'Tom made this elephant and he called it Nellie' (written by a nursery child, with the teacher's support, as a label for his model elephant), or 'This is a red car and My mummy likes it' (a caption accompanying a reception child's picture, see chapter 4). The texts can be longer with strings of observations plus comments. It is a genre familiar to primary teachers and one that is ranked highly when different pieces of writing are evaluated. Interestingly, it is not a genre that is used much by adults, except perhaps on postcards or in letters. In fact, expression of personal feelings is considered unacceptable in many kinds of writing where observations are made. Science reports, for example, will be criticized in a child's later school years if personal references are made.

Why do children write in this way? Martin and Rothery argue that the answer lies in the teacher–child interactions. Writing development activities encourage children, first, to write more as they grow older. The label 'This is a . . .' is not considered enough once the child moves up the school. Secondly, the types of questions used by the teacher encourage the child to add some personal comment. Some evidence for this comes from the earlier example of classroom practice (see chapter 5) where the teacher supported children's development as writers by helping them talk about their chosen topics. Here, the teacher was encouraging the children to add a comment to their observation. The writing produced by Michael (fig. 5.4) following the teacher's intervention was of the observation/comment genre and was evaluated as an 'improved' example of writing.

Martin (1984) suggests that this desire to elicit a personal reaction from the child reflects deeply held notions about the child's development of self and about the need for writing to be creative and authentic:

Britton's description of expressive writing as the foundation of writing of other kinds; Graves' emphasis on ownership, and a number of other literary and psychoanalytic threads conspire to promote the inclusion of feeling in texts (Martin, 1984, p. 3)

From this early genre of observation/comment two different types of writing are identified in Martin and Rothery's survey. These are 'recount' and 'report'. In turn, these are the foundations of two main generic strands of development: recount leading to the development of narrative genres and report leading to expository genres.

Recount is characterized as sequences of events often connected by 'and then' or with an implicit 'then'. Rothery (1984, pp. 72–3) gives the following example of a recount from an eight-year-old:

I went to the zoo. I saw the snake and the [sic] I saw the boa constrictor it was big and thick and the colour was green and brown. Then we went to the koala house and the baby koala and then we went down and then we went to see the seals and one fat one did not go in the water then we went to see the elephant and we gave him some biscuits with vegemite and we went to the lions and the lion was brown We went to get the Ferry and we sang and we sang Yellow Bird Mrs Green sang too. We sang Mr Postman and then the boat then we went to catch the train and we went home.

This recount has an initial orientation (I went to the zoo) and a reorientation (We went home) with a series of of temporally ordered events in between. It is thus, genre theorists argue, similar in structure to narrative except that there is no disruption in the sequence, no unexpected turn of events. True narratives appear later and are marked by an orientation – complication – resolution structure, for example, as in:

Once upon a time there was a dragon that laughed at everything. One day another dragon roared and roared and the dragon that thought everything was funny laughed and laughed. He laughed so much that he died of laughing. (Manchester Infant)

Examples of narrative did not appear in Martin and Rothery's sample until the third year of primary school, although significantly most teachers classed all the writing of younger children as stories. Narrative is given a very central place in primary schools both in what children are expected to read and have read to them and in what they are expected to write. 'Write a story about what happened . . .' is a frequent directive after an outing or an event. The type of questioning that teachers use when discussing a child's ideas for writing such as 'So what happened next?' often lead children towards narrative. It is perhaps not surprising that in schools where the writing curriculum has been radically changed in many ways such that children have different purposes and audiences for their writing, narrative remains dominant, with stories for younger children topping the list of writing activities. But despite this popularity for narrative, the actual structural nature of narrative is rarely made explicit to children. They are left to acquire narrative forms through their reading and through occasional clues from the teacher's comments, such as 'I liked the ending but what happened to the Happy Hippo?'

When direct guidance is given, it has proved successful. An example from the National Writing Project comes from the work of Roger Mulley and Margaret Axford who wanted to help children shape their experiences into narrative forms. First, they took popular examples of narrative where there was clear disruption of events (e.g. Jill Murphy's *On the Way Home*) and discussed them with the children. Then they introduced a storyboard technique which encouraged children to draft their stories in picture sequences, then to talk through the storyline and finally to write the narrative (NWP, 1989a). The combination of narrative focus and the opportunity to rehearse the story, first in pictures, then in talk, seemed to help the children structure their experience more effectively.

Some would go further than to question the level of guidance given about the nature of narrative and challenge the dominant position of this particular genre. Martin (1984), for example, suggests that the bias towards narrative has serious social consequences. First, it limits children's experience of those forms of expository writing that are highly valued in secondary school, a consequence that may affect girls in particular whose high achievements in writing narrative in primary school count for little when they are judged by different standards in subject-based secondary curricula. Secondly, by promoting narrative, Martin suggests that children are denied access to the kind of writing needed to take some control over their lives: 'It imprisons them in a world of fantasy and make-believe which their society deems appropriate for sub-adults.'

Such an argument is in sharp contrast to those encouraging narrative as a means through which children can learn to express their feelings and explore their world.

While narrative dominates, factual writing also develops in primary schools. In Martin and Rothery's survey, children frequently produced reports which are factual accounts of observed events. These differ from recounts in that they are not ordered temporally (i.e. you cannot insert 'then' between each sentence). A second-year Infant in a Manchester school, for example, produced the following report after a visit to the 'wild area':

We went to the wild area today and the board was not there. The slugs used to live under the board. Because it is beginning to be Winter in the wild area there was some frost. We found a carton a cloth and some leaves. The carton was covered in frost. Mr Smith is going to make a pond out of the hole in the wild area after Christmas. The ice was melting because the sun came out.

The report genre provides the structural foundation for the later development of the expository genre with its characteristic structure of classification and description (see below). This genre is the one highly valued in much later school writing. Reports seem to be favoured by boys more than girls, a reflection, no doubt, of their preferred reading habits. But while reports are encouraged by certain writing tasks in primary schools, such as descriptions of places visited, the writing produced tends not to be as highly valued as other types. This may be due to the teacher's bias towards personal feeling and originality which are less likely to be included in the report. Teachers need to ensure that narrative yardsticks are not being used to measure the success of expository writing.

The report and narrative genres are very different and need to be judged on their own terms. The question is not whether a narrative is more imaginative or creative and sincere than a report, but whether or not the narrative is a good narrative and the report is an effective report. At this point a longish word needs to be said about 'genre' in order for the educational arguments to develop further.

Genre theory

The concept of 'genre'is an important one in recent discussions about the writing curriculum and one that is at the centre of many heated debates (e.g. Reid, 1987). Genre theory developed in Australia from the work of Michael Halliday. His theory of systemic linguistics provides a view of language in which words and sentences are seen to be patterned and organized to achieve different purposes and meanings. In our culture, there are many familiar patterned variants or genres in both speech and writing. For instance, the following is a typical classroom spoken genre:

Right then, what's happening there?
The man's washing.
Yes, anyone else? What's he washing?
He's washing the baby.
Good, he's bathing the baby.

It is not hard to suggest a context for this extract, nor to identify the likely speakers. The different roles of children and teacher are known and each participant chooses from a particular vocabulary. For example, it is the teacher who says 'good'/'right then'; and it is the teacher who asks most questions, questions to which she knows, and the children know that she knows, the answers.

Within the group of classroom genres, one could typify a curriculum genre for the process-based approach such as: discussion – drafting – conferencing – revision – editing – publishing. In a similar way, recognizable sequences could be given for a visit to the doctor; a conversation with a stranger at the bus stop and so on. The exchanges are not fixed but they tend to fall into accepted patterns, the most convincing evidence of which comes in our ability to 'send up' the activities in amusing ways. The existence of recognizable patterned variants of language use is necessary to help people know how to behave. Arguably, they also promote the most effective use of language to achieve particular ends. For example, questions are a necessary and effective means for a doctor to reach a reliable diagnosis of the problem. Of course, particular variants may also serve to establish power relations which may need to be challenged.

In writing, as in speech, different types of texts can be seen to have particular patterns. So, we can describe the structure of a story, an argument or a letter to the bank manager. (Though how many distinct structural variants or genres there are is still open to discussion.) In learning to write, children are involved in learning to recognize and learn the different ways in which meanings are shaped in written texts. That is, they are learning to control the different genres. Often, it is argued (e.g. Christie, 1984), that schools fail to show pupils explicitly what the nature of each genre is, leaving children to work them out for themselves through their reading and through the few clues given by the teachers in their general instructions (e.g. 'remember to write a beginning, middle and end') and their evaluative comments (e.g. 'a good report, but where's your conclusion?'). Furthermore, the argument goes, teachers are often unaware of the types of writing they are teaching. Nor are they aware of their implicit ranking of different genres in order of importance, which can result in children getting better marks for some bits of writing than for others but without their ever knowing why.

An analysis of two genres

Christie provides two examples of children's texts to demonstrate what is meant by 'genre: a purposeful, staged, cultural activity'. The first is a familiar type of school text which Christie suggests can be classified as an example of the 'expository genre'. It was written by 12-year-old Rebecca in her first year at secondary school (figure 8.1). The second was written by 11-year-old Terry who, as part of a class activity, was asked to write and illustrate a story for younger children in the school (see figure 8.2). The questions Christie asks are: what were the writer's purposes for the different pieces of

Drugs.

These are some of the illegal drugs which are around Opium, Heroin, Marijuana and Anoigesics. All are taken by many senceless and childish people all over the world. I belive people get involved in drugs for many reasons ; one unimployment, unhappyness, influence from friends, problems at home, they think they are tough and important and also the think they are grow up.

Drug addiction is when someone gets hooked on drugs and they find it impossible to get of them. Many people get addicted by having more so that they can cope with life. This con do many awfull and terrifying things to you body system. Many of the effects can be fattle. They can make you psychological or physiological or in some cases both, it can also affect the nervous system in your body. I think people that take drugs are very silly. When I grow up I hope I will not smoke drink or take drugs I am going to sign of those forms to say that I will not do those three things (smoke drink or take drugs). I think that every person the deals in drugs ought to be hugh because of some of the terrifing things it doese to people it is skadless.

Figure 8.1   *Rebecca: example of expository genre.*
Source: F. Christie 1984: Varieties of written discourse. In *Deakin University Course Study Guide: Children Writing*. Victoria: Deakin University, p. 13.

Figure 8.2

Figure 8.2 *Terry: example of story writing for younger children.*
Source: F. Christie 1984: Varieties of written discourse. In *Deakin University Course Study Guide: Children Writing*. Victoria: Deakin University, pp. 16–17.

writing? How successful are they in achieving their aims? And how do you know the answers to these questions?

Analysis of the structure of Rebecca's text shows that she is aware and able to handle fairly competently an argumentative essay. The text has a recognizable ordered sequence of steps. It begins with an introduction, then some exposition, an attempted definition, a personal observation and a conclusion.

The whole essay has an authoritative feel to it: 'she understands that particular kinds of purposes are served in writing essays, and hence that meanings are constructed and organised in ways particular to the essay genre' (1984, p. 15). Christie provides a schematic structure for the text (table 8.1).

Terry's story for younger children similarly reveals a knowledge of a particular genre, this time of story structure. The order and development of the text are very different from Rebecca's exposition. There is an introduction, in which the time, character and the problem are established. This is followed by a complication, then a resolution and finally a coda, or comment. Christie's analysis is shown in table 8.2. Again, the structural analysis shows the child's control of the genre. In this case it includes the control of the illustrations so that they support the story's unfolding. In contrast, Rebecca's illustrations seem to add nothing and are of questionable appropriateness.

In broad terms, the comparison of these two types of text reveals the culturally accepted characteristics of an expository and a narrative genre. Typically, in the narrative genre, information is set out and ordered in a manner reflecting the unfolding of events over time. It is usually in the past tense. In contrast, the expository genre typically orders information in ways that make considerations of reason and argument more important than considerations of time and space. It is usually in the present tense. These categorizations do not exclude the possibility of using a narrative genre with an ordered sequence of events over time to provide say an argument against the use of drugs (after all, that is the purpose of fables and parables). Nor do they exclude the possibility of, say, using present tense in narratives.

While the use of genres for different purposes is not fixed, this does not negate the claim that texts have characteristic organizations and schematic structures which allow different meanings to be made. If I choose to write to my bank manager about my overdraft in the form of a witty poem rather than a formal letter, I will have shaped the words differently and conveyed a very different meaning (and may well get a different response).

Table 8.1   *Schematic structure of Rebecca's text*

Stage 1. Rebecca introduces a variety of drugs.	'These are some of the illegal drugs which are around Opium, Heroin, Marijuana and Analgesics.'
Stage 2. She comments on some of the reasons why people take them.	'All are taken by many senceless and childish people all over the world. I believe people get involved in drugs for many reasons; one unemployment, unhappyness, influence from friends, problems at home, they think they are tough and important and also the think they are grow up.'
Stage 3. She defines drug addiction and refers to the debilitating effects of taking drugs.	'Drug addiction is when someone gets hooked on drugs and they find it impossible to get of them. Many people get addicted by having more so they can cope with life. This can do many awfull and terrifing things to you body system. Many of the effects can be fattle. They can make you psychological or physiological or in some cases both, it can also affect the nervous system in your body.'
Stage 4. She offers her own judgement on persons who take drugs.	'I think people that take drugs are very silly. When I grow up I hope I will not smoke drink or take drugs. I am going to sign of those forms to say I will not do those three things (smoke, drink or take drugs).'
Stage 5. She offers a concluding judgement on drug dealers.	'I think that every person the deals in drugs ought to be hugh[a] because of some of the terrifing things it does to people it is skadless[b].'

[a] hung.
[b] scandalous.
Source: F. Christie 1984: Varieties of written discourse. In *Deakin University Course Study Guide: Children Writing*. Victoria: Deakin University, p. 14.

Table 8.2   *Structural analysis of Terry's story*

Stage 1. The main character is introduced in his setting and his problem identified.	'One day Timmy the clock was in the store window. No one would buy him because he was shy. Every time people looked at him, he would set off his alarm, until he bounced around to face the other way. He always did this because he didn't like the looks of the people.'
Stage 2. A second character is introduced and a complication arises.	'One day a little girl came past, and he didn't put his alarm on. He liked her very much, but then she went away. Timmy was sad because he had liked that girl.'
Stage 3. The complication is resolved.	'The next day the girl came back again. He was so happy that he put on his alarm and started jumping for joy. The little girl bought him and he was so happy.'
Stage 4. A final comment on the character of Timmy and his relationship to the other character is offered.	'But he was still shy. Every time some one looked at him, he would put on his alarm and turn around. Except when the girl looked at him.

Source: F. Christie 1984: Varieties of written discourse. In *Deakin University Course Study Guide: Children Writing*. Victoria: Deakin University, p. 18.

The description of the two children's texts is more than a linguistic exercise. It raises central questions about how the children learned to write like this (and how others often fail to) and how teachers can support such learning. The children may not be consciously aware of the structured sequences they are employing, though they may be able to talk about the discussions they had with the teacher and about the influences of their reading experiences. But however conscious the language choices are, they are learned understandings about language, something much more than an 'intuitive feel' for writing or a 'personal voice'. Here is the process versus genre rub: if control of different varieties of writing involves specific learned writing behaviours, then, the genre theorists argue, the nature of these behaviours should be known to the teacher who can monitor and assess their development. This would involve the teacher paying specific attention to linguistic structures used in order to discuss how successful Terry and Rebecca were in their writing. Genre theory provides a means of identifying the language organization of different texts.

Terry and Rebecca's texts: a close analysis

I felt that Terry's story was more effective than Rebecca's. Of course, you cannot directly compare them as they are different structures so I should say more accurately that I felt that Terry's was a good example of story-writing, while Rebecca's did not seem such a good example of argumentative essay. Why? At a text level they both seemed to have produced coherently organized passages. The difference seems to lie in the children's control of what systemic linguists call the 'context'. By context is meant the circumstances under which the language interaction takes place: that is, what's being talked about (the field of discourse); who's taking part and how the participants related to each other (the tenor), and what channel of communication is being used (the mode).

In Rebecca's writing, the field of discourse is drugs and their effects on people. To write effectively about these, Rebecca needs to be able to draw on an appropriate vocabulary about drugs and knowledge about what drugs do to people. A close look at her writing shows that Rebecca has a rather limited number of lexical items about drugs to draw on. For instance, her descriptions of the effects are vague like 'This can do many awfull and terrifing things' or inaccurate as in 'They can make you psychological or physiological.' Likewise, her opinion about drugs reveals her inexperience with the subject which leads her to sentences like 'I think people who take drugs are very silly'. Christie concludes after looking at Rebecca's text:

. . . the analysis has shown why the text fails to satisfy as a convincing piece of writing. The writer is not in control of a sufficiently precise or extensive lexis relevant to the field of drugs. The point is an important one, for writing efforts such as Rebecca's are frequently misunderstood or dismissed because teachers do not make accurate judgements about them and the comments they offer children are therefore often not helpful.

Commonly, texts such as Rebecca's would invite comments such as 'poor ideas', 'poorly organised', 'poorly argued', or 'poorly expressed'. In fact, the text is very well organised . . . There is, in addition, not much wrong with the expression, because with some exceptions she writes in appropriate sentences. Her problem is not 'poor ideas': close examination of her lexis reveals lack of information on the subject. (Christie, 1984, p. 27)

In comparison, the story by Terry seems to include appropriate vocabulary for describing the passage of time, Timmy's feelings and the little girl's actions. Not only is the choice of words appropriate but also the words to do with time, feelings and actions are distributed within the text in a way that provides a sense of unity. It is an easy text to read not simply because it is a young child's story but because the text coheres through the vocabulary choices.

If we look at the 'tenor' of the two pieces, further differences emerge in the successful control of the two genres exhibited by the children. Tenor refers to the relationship between the participants in the interaction. Typical of the expository argument, for example, is the use of the third person and the avoidance of personal observations. This is not a necessary condition of a good argument, but one that tends to be the accepted practice, particularly in school writing tasks. Rebecca, however, uses the first person quite frequently and talks about personal experiences 'When I grow up I hope I will not smoke drink or take drugs.' Overall her text suggests that she is unsure what tone to adopt with her audience: an authoritative account of drugs (which her limited knowledge must make her uneasy about adopting), or a friendly conversation about her feelings (which fits uneasily into the written mode). Terry, on the other hand, seems to appreciate the tenor of story writing for younger children. The third person is consistently used with no noticeable intrusion of the author's real identity. Perhaps this confidence is not surprising given his years of experience of reading similar stories.

The third factor identified as affecting the genre is 'mode' of communication, that is, whether it is oral or written, a conversation, a lecture, a telephone call or a Fax. The mode will affect the language choices as has been discussed in chapter 2. With respect to the two texts, both were designed to be written, though Terry's seems to have been successfully structured so that it could be read aloud to a younger child. Such a choice would probably not have been considered for Rebecca's piece. It is interesting to observe in passing that school practice generally encourages arguments to be written in essay form even though children's experiences of arguments outside school – on TV, at home, in the streets – are likely to be oral exchanges.

It might appear that genre theory is rather involved and technical. But this is where the core of the genre school's argument lies. Language is complex and needs to be recognized and understood as such. If we obscure the complexity by letting children discover it for themselves, relying on guesswork and their own informal analysis of other people's writing during their reading, we are doing a disservice to children's struggles to acquire the cultural practices of writing. Teachers need to be explicit in their evaluations of texts and to appreciate the demands they are making.

The genre debate

The perspective on the writing curriculum developed by genre theorists opens up new questions about the contexts for writing that different activities provide. The way in which each writing task is set up will have consequences for children's ability to control the appropriate genre in terms of what is said, how it is said and in what medium. Such consequences have been recognized in curriculum innovations which stress the importance of providing a purpose and audience for writing. Genre theory argues that children also need support in learning the *forms* of writing expected of them for different audiences and purposes. It is not enough to have a 'real' reason for writing and a 'real' person to write for, children also need to be helped to understand the 'real' ways in which writing can be formed. New emphasis is placed on the text itself and teachers are asked to interrogate how well the child has managed a particular functional variant of writing through analysis of the written products. Put another way, genre theory places language structures firmly in the curriculum picture.

The criticisms that are levelled against the genre school are mainly in terms of their pedagogical implications if taken to a particular extreme. The main attack has come from the 'process-based' exponents who fear that a genre approach, with its emphasis on children learning different types of writing, will threaten children's freedom to express their personal feelings, to find their own 'voice'. They conjure up pictures of children learning written variants in teacher-controlled language lessons, with no quarter given to purposes and audiences. The debate has been emotionally and ideologically charged with protagonists taking up extreme views which sometimes seem a far cry from actual classroom practice.

A flavour of the debate can be had in the accusation that genre theory will result in restrictions on children's choice of what to write, and thus constrain their ability to express themselves in their own words. Martin et al. (1987) counterattack by asking what freedom is there when 'free choice' of topic and 'free choice' of written form results in every child producing either recounts or stories throughout their primary schooling?

The teachers do not create choices for [the children] so they do not have choices to take up. Offering choices in [process] classrooms . . . is not enabling. It is pseudo-choice. Writers cannot take up options they do not have. (Quoted in Reid, 1987, p. 77)

In order to have freedom and power over language, children need guidance about how meanings can be shaped through language. Direction from the teacher about how different written varieties function in the culture to convey different meanings provides the necessary scaffolding to support children's development as writers. This is not an intrusion on the child's ability to express her or himself but a way of demonstrating the opportunities available beyond the stereotypes too often resorted to.

Certainly this argument is intuitively appealing and one that brings back memories of my own school days where generic guidance was not in evidence. When reading various articles from the 'genre' school, I found myself remembering in vivid detail an experience I had in my first year of secondary school. The English curriculum was of a traditional kind with lessons devoted to 'composition', 'literature' and 'grammar'. Once a week we were asked to write, for homework, on a topic of our choice. I was considered a good writer but not brilliant. No one ever told me why I did not reach the prized A/A+ grades. One week, I sat for ages trying to think of a suitable writing topic and felt empty of ideas. In frustration, I just began writing with the words 'I sucked my pen and stared out of the window. It was a lovely day. . . .' I forget the details but remember that it took on dreamlike qualities with me wandering around the countryside and ended with me waking up and finding myself staring at an empty exercise book. This might not sound particularly original but, in the context of our English lessons, it was a radical venture. I gave the book in for marking, feeling nervous that I would be reprimanded for frivolous use of composition time. The book came back and there in red was my first 'A+'. I remember wondering whether I had discovered latent writing talents, or whether I had simply got away with something.

I don't know why this one event stays so clearly in my mind. Perhaps it was because I got close to finding out what it was that the teacher valued most highly. Sadly, though, my achievements were never explained to me and my writing development continued along its haphazard path. Like countless schoolchildren, the forms of language I was to learn in school depended not on any explicit instruction but on my reading (predominantly narrative) and any messages I could pick up from the grades and comments. My learning about different genres was left to chance and, like many writers, I am aware that what I write often fails, through lack of effective structure, to achieve its intended purpose.

Many examples come to mind of children's texts (or adults' come to that) which lack generic guidance. But decisions about generic focus or lack of it cannot be made lightly. Who is to say which text is most generically sound? Who is the arbiter of a good report, a good letter to the bank manager? There can be no clear answers to such questions. Genre theorists run the risk of creating a genre orthodoxy in which they have predetermined what it is that children should have learned to write.

Martin et al. (1987), for example, give the following text which, they argue, typifies writing that lacks generic focus. The text accompanied a series of photographs of children making toast:

All the things are on the table. We will use them to make toast. There is honey, vegemite, peanut butter, bread, margarine, jam, a knife, a plate and a toaster. We are ready to make toast. Kevin is getting two slices of bread out of the packet. Then he puts the bread in the toaster. The bread goes down automatically with a spring. The element starts to get hot and red. Kevin puts his hand over the toaster to feel how hot the toaster was. The control switch makes the bread brown. Kevin watches the bread inside the toaster cooking. It is still white. The toast came popping out. Jean is getting the toast out of the toaster. The bread has gone brown. Jean had to be careful because of the electricity and also because the toaster was hot. (Quoted in Reid, 1987, p. 72)

The genre theorists provide a critique of this text as follows:

This kind of writing is not functional in our culture. Generically speaking it is neither recount (i.e. what we did) nor procedure (i.e. how to do something). And the mode is wrong: parts of the text read like a running commentary on the photos scaffolding the field. But running commentaries are spoken not written down. Even this is inconsistent, as can be demonstrated by examining the number of tenses used: are (present); will use (future); is getting (present in present) came (past); has gone (past in present). Moreover running commentary makes use of (present in present) tense for actions. But actions [here] are usually the 'timeless' (present) characteristic of reports: puts, goes, starts, puts, makes (not is putting, is going, is starting etc.) This is not just a case of mixing up tenses. Tenses like the rest of grammar are functional, they are designed to mean. Rather the inconsistency of tense selection is symptomatic of the lack of generic focus given by the teacher to the negotiation. The teacher had no clear social purpose in mind. (Quoted in Reid, 1987, p. 72)

This analysis raises critical questions about the extent to which genre theory will provide the elusive 'freedom' for the writer. Martin et al. are quite categorical in rejecting the text as 'not functional' in our culture. But whose culture are they talking about? While it is not a type of writing that I find appealing, it is one that is familiar from various reading schemes, albeit with a few tense slippages. I would also imagine that it would be recognized by many teachers as having an intended social purpose of providing children with a 'language experience' based text to support their reading. Such texts frequently are in the form of written running commentary. (Though I would imagine that most primary school teachers would edit this text heavily to remove references to Kevin's hands on the toaster!)

Few deny the importance of looking at how well children have acquired different written variants, or even making everyday implicit evaluations of 'good' genre examples more explicit to children. What is worrying is if categorical statements are made about what genres are acceptable and what are not or about the major genres necessary for all children to learn in order to meet society's writing demands. The danger is that such judgements can be turned into a writing policy whereby each child practises the required genre until an agreed level of proficiency is reached. The theory that claims that many children are being disenfranchised in writing by not being shown how different forms of writing are structured, could, with a slight twist to the argument, become a recipe for a very traditional curriculum of genre transmission; each child being required to learn the dominant forms of writing, thus reinforcing inequalities of class and sex. Green (1987) puts this extreme view like this:

[genre theory] could be interpreted . . . as a complicity in the cultural task of schooling, viewed as a means of (re)producing the dominant, hegemonic culture, including the 'proper' order of gendered identities and relations. (Quoted in Reid, 1987, p. 86)

While such a pedagogical consequence was certainly not intended by the main developers of the genre school, it is a risk if genres are treated as though they are fixed, with no development possible within or across genres. A particular genre may have evolved in a way that best supports the shaping of meaning for a particular area of knowledge; for example, an impersonal report may be a more effective way of conveying information about a scientific experiment than a story would be. But this should not exclude the possibility that a narrative genre may sometimes serve a purpose in science reports or that, at a different time, the report genre may be very different from its current accepted structure. What appears to be needed to avoid genre theory constraining children's choice of written variety is more emphasis on the historical development of different genre and more discussion among children and teachers of why they are selecting a particular genre for a particular purpose. The writing curriculum needs to provide opportunities for children to recognize and discuss the cultural practices that affect what and how we write.

9

Knowing about Writing

The previous chapter with its very specific focus on a few pieces of writing produced by children in writing classrooms may seem a long way away from the opening chapter on the nature of literacy. But they have in common a deep concern about the knowledge that teachers should have about writing. This book began with questions about our knowledge of literacy: how much do we know about the different uses of writing practised by the children inside and outside school? The evidence presented from ethnographic studies reveals that 'school literacy' represents only a small range of 'ways of taking' practised in different communities. Genre theory, as described in the previous chapter, focuses specifically on our knowledge about the 'ways of taking' in school writing environments. What are the linguistic options that children have in their use of language? How well can we evaluate their ability to use different forms of writing? Both the broader social perspective and the narrower linguistic one are concerned with the ways in which meaning is realized through language, how language imposes an order on our thinking and attitudes. Both question the extent to which education provides different groups with equal access to literacy. The conclusion that both reach is that teachers and children need to have a greater awareness of how literacy is used and how texts are structured. One way to exemplify these statements is to look at the role of language in one specific subject area: science.

Language and science

Each subject shapes its meaning through the language varieties it uses, and the task of the writer is to take the information
given in the lesson and work it into the appropriate pattern.
But, too often, discovery of how the different subjects' meanings are to be realized in texts is left to chance. Those who
fail in a particular subject may have failed to use the clues
from their reading or from teacher directions to work out the
written discourse through which the 'knowledge' of a subject
is arranged. Sometimes children make a pretty good guess at
the language variety they should adopt for a particular subject
as demonstrated by an 11-year-old in figure 9.1.

Teachers have been aware that language can prove the stum-
bling block to children's understanding of a subject. But that
awareness is usually centred around children's misconcep-
tions about the meanings of particular words. Common
examples include children's misconstruction of words such
as 'vacuum' (something that sucks) or evaporated (a milky
substance), where they have used their personal experience
of words to derive a related but inadequate understanding of
technical concepts. Beyond the word level, researchers such
as Perera (1981, 1984) have demonstrated the difficulties children face with certain linguistic structures. Examples include
phrases and clauses that are coordinated or subordinated in
ways not common in children's language. For instance 'or'
and 'if' are used in unusual ways in the following extracts
from school textbooks:

And so the electric current, *or*, the rate at which the electrons are
flowing, must be the same all round the circuit.

If there was not much daylight, neither were there many ways of
providing artificial light. (From Perera, 1984)

But while such examples reveal the potential hazards facing
young readers and writers, they tend to make subject-based
language seem problematic rather than to highlight how

<u>Experment</u>
<u>Aim</u>: to look at the effect of chemical
energy
Method:
    <u>Equiptment</u>
One small testle tude and stopper

I spectular
baking soda (sodium bicartonate dilate
acetic
  petroteam jelly

Place 0.5cm of baking soda in a
test tube over sink poenting away
from you. Add one cm of add Place
the greased stopper in the test tube

<u>Result</u>: when we put in all the chemical
the lid poped off
<u>Conclusion</u> - I look at the effect of
chemical ennergy

Figure 9.1 *An 11-year-old's science 'recipe'.*
Source: J. White (in collaboration with G. Welford) 1987: *The Language of Science: Making and Interpreting Observations*. Report prepared for the Assessment of Performance Unit, Department of Education and Science, London: HMSO.

subjects attempt to use linguistic structures to achieve particular ends. For instance, the tendency in much scientific language to avoid personal references and to use the passive rather than active voice is sometimes seen as an unnecessary feature, designed to exclude all but an elite from the subject. However, it can be argued that the choice of particular linguistic structures serves useful purposes. The use of passives, for instance, allows the focus of the sentence, the theme, to be on the significant part of the experiment rather than on the less important (scientifically speaking) participants. Thus 'Magnesium was added to the solution' focuses the reader's attention on the aspects of the account considered most important. In contrast, 'We added magnesium' moves the focus away from the scientific event. The linguistic structures used in different subject areas impose a specific order on the subject.

White (1987) in a report for the Assessment of Performance Unit looks at the language of science texts and at children's ability to control the appropriate discourse. She argues that attention to the forms of language used in different subjects is not an optional extra at any level of text construction. How words, sentences and larger chunks of language are ordered depends on the communicative purpose and context.

We need to look at whole stretches of language, at whole texts, to discover what kind of understandings a speaker or writer is attempting to convey in the context of any communicative activity. (White, 1987, p. 11)

Two contrasting responses of 15-year-olds to a task in the APU language survey demonstrate how language structures reality. The task was to study two pictures of demoiselle flies, fly A and fly B, to note differences and to write an account which would emphasize significant differences. Two high scoring texts are given in figures 9.2 and 9.3. White commends the originality and effective style of the fictional narrative text, but goes on to show the constraints imposed on the author by this choice of genre:

It is one of those lazy hot days in summer when everything is warm and very quiet. The trees surrounding the lake at the bottom of the hill are swaying silently and the ripples on the lake give the impression of peace and tranquillity.

At the end of the lake are reeds and lilies. Flies buzz dozily among the tall grasses, look for food. Bees laze among the pollen filled lilies, drinking their sweet nectar and the demoiselle flies perch motionless on the tall green fronds of the reeds.

There are two in particular, one male, one female, that catch my eye as I lie against the sturdy trunk of an ancient oak. They are the most beautiful creatures I have ever seen, but they are *both* different.

One has lacy wings, so clear I can see the water's edge through them. Its colouring is of brilliant pinks and blues, and it stands out amongst the yellow buttercups that surround it. Its abdomen is long, like a finger, and incredibly thin. It looks so fragile, as though any sudden movement may snap it, like a twig. Its lacy wings stretch back, almost to the full length of the abdomen, like delicate fans, cooling its body. Its head is small but bold. It is completely blue with piercing black eyes on either side of its head. The legs of this magnificent creature are long and black, with what look like hairs of the finest thread, placed at even spaces down each side.

The thorax, the part next to its head, is large. It is not as slender as the abdomen, but it is very sleek, with patches of blue and black reflecting the brilliant sunlight.

As I watch, its head rotates and then suddenly it has disappeared, hovering over the lake.

The other demoiselle fly still remains. This is not such a beautiful creature as the first, but it has striking markings. The wings are a dull brown in colour. They are much wider and not as long. They appear to be much more powerful than the lacy, delicate wings of the other fly. The abdomen of this creature is much thicker. It is dull brown, like the wings, but has flecks

Figure 9.2

of mauve and grey. It appears, just as with the wings, to be much stronger, more substantial, and more useful.

The legs are very thick, although they still have that same appearance of delicacy about them, with the thin hairs vibrating rhythmically. The thorax is not as long as that of the other fly, but is much thicker and more developed. It is green in colour with touches of brown, and gives the impression of strong armour plating.

The head is noble and bold. It is held high and the eyes are much larger and more powerful looking. It appears that this creature would be the male, as he appears stronger and more masculine in his appearance.

He waits, motionless for a few seconds, then hovers over the lake, searching for the other fly, then disappears.

I am now left alone by the waters edge, the sun beating down, the flies once again busy in their search for food.

Figure 9.2   *Comparative description of demoiselle flies (writer aged 15):*
narrative form.
Source: J. White (in collaboration with G. Welford) 1987: *The Language of Science: Making and Interpreting Observations.* Report prepared for the Assessment of Performance Unit, Department of Education and Science, London: HMSO.

The script demonstrates some of the ways in which commitment to a first person narrative mode actually obscures some of the clarity of observed detail which the 'story' contains, despite itself. For example, the opening paragraphs are an excursion into pure fantasy, which however original in conception as a starting point for the description, are redolent with fairly well-known cliches (lazy hot days, ripples on the lake, pollen filled lilies . . .). From this conventional evocation of summer it is not surprising that the general adjective for describing the damsel fly turns out to be the minimally informative 'beautiful'. In the same lexical range are other descriptors: 'magnificent', 'powerful', 'noble' and 'bold'. The progressive humanising of the flies leads to the inaccurate description of what is visible; 'wings are much wider and not as long' (in fact A's wings are a quarter as wide again as B's but the same length) 'abdomen

The demoiselle fly in general has a short thorax long abdomen and bulbous compound eyes.

Type A has all the aforementioned mentioned qualities but differs from type B in the following ways:

1. It has six long black legs with long hairs on top and lower parts of its leg's. Type B only has four leg's and has hair's on the bottom of its forelegs and top of its hindlegs only.

2. Type A has opaque wing's which are short and wide. Type B has transparent wings which are notably longer and thinner than type A's.

3. Type A has it's abdomen segmented into fairly small parts, the end section tapering to a point. Type B has it's abdomen made up of fairly small parts the end part tapering downwards to make it triangular.

4. The most notable difference between the two is their markings. Type A is Brown and green on it's thorax, having brown wing's which get lighter towards the edges and a brown abdomen. Type B is light blue and light brown on its thorax having colourless wing's apart from 3 brown spots on the end of it's wings and a blue brown and black abdomen with just a tinge of pink all over it.

5. Type A's eyes are brown, and bisected laterally with a jagged line. Type B's are blue (pale) with a black spot in the centre.

6. Type A has pointed mandibles but type B's is box shaped.

Figure 9.3 *Comparative description of demoiselle flies (writer aged 15): scientific form.*
Source: J. White (in collaboration with G. Welford) 1987: *The Language of Science: Making and Interpreting Observations*. Report prepared for the Assessment of Performance Unit, Department of Education and Science, London: HMSO.

much thicker' (the abdomens are the same size), 'legs very thick' (infinitesimally different), 'eyes much larger' (same size). (White, 1987)

Narrative, it seems, is not a written form that is best suited to a task such as this where precise descriptions are required.

The other text is scientifically ordered, though itself not entirely error free (e.g. B's wings are not noticeably longer than A's). The structural order allows major differences to be presented, though the author has not fully exploited the order of points, putting the 'most notable' in fourth place. Other criticisms are possible, but it can be seen how the text has a structure in which the major differences could be effectively communicated.

This is not to suggest that children should be given templates for writing in different subjects nor that they should be discouraged from using their 'own words'. What is being argued is that the language choice available should be discussed and that children should be explicitly aware of the freedoms and constraints of different language forms. Their explorations of scientific concepts should be accompanied by explorations of ways of articulating what they have learned according to the purpose and audience of their communication.

Teachers need to see language issues as integral to the child's understanding of all subjects. Writing and talking about a subject are not simply end products of work done in class; they are the realization of a child's learning.

Endnote

Awareness of language is of central importance to the teacher. As the science example demonstrates, the knowledge that is needed goes far beyond spelling rules and grammatical niceties like how to avoid split infinitives. The knowledge needed rests on reflections about the way children and teachers interact in different writing environments and on evaluation of the range of literacy experiences provided. Knowing about writing involves learning about the literacy experiences of children in their homes and communities. With regard to school writing activities, it involves learning and talking about what it means to be a writer and how writing varies according to the purposes and audience of the text. Alongside such general understandings of literacy practices and processes, must come study – both explicitly through discussion and implicitly through the design of the curriculum – of the language used itself. Whenever we write we are making choices, choices which form our experiences. Children need to know as much as possible about these choices and so be able to develop (and challenge) their literacy heritage.

Bibliography

Bereiter, C. and Scardamalia, M. 1985: From conversation to composition. In *Deakin University Course Reader: Children Writing*. Victoria: Deakin University, pp. 106–34.

Bissex, G. 1980: *Gnys at Wrk: a Child Learns to Read and Write*. Cambridge, Mass.: Harvard University Press.

Bloomfield, L. 1935: *Language*. London: George, Allen and Unwin.

Britton, J., Burgess, T., Martin, N., McLeod, A. and Rosen, H. 1975: *The Development of Writing Abilities (11–18)*. London: Macmillan.

Bruner, J. 1986: *Actual Minds, Possible Worlds*. Cambridge, Mass.: Harvard University Press.

Chafe, W. L. 1982: Integration and involvement in speaking, writing and oral literature. In D. Tannen (ed.): *Spoken and Written Language*. Norwood, NJ: Ablex.

Chafe, W. L. 1985: Linguistic differences produced by differences between speaking and writing. In D. R. Olson, N. Torrance and A. Hildyard (eds): *Literacy, Language and Learning. The Nature and Consequences of Reading and Writing*. Cambridge: Cambridge University Press, pp. 105–23.

Christie, F. 1984: Varieties of written discourse. In *Deakin University Course Study Guide: Children Writing*. Victoria: Deakin University.

Christie, F. 1987: Genres as choice. In I. Reid (ed.): *The Place of Genre in Learning: Current Debates*. Centre for Studies in Literary Education: Deakin University, Victoria, pp. 22–34.

Clay, M. 1975: *What Did I Write?* London: Heinemann Educational Books.

Cook-Gumperz, J. (ed.) 1986: *The Social Construction of Literacy*. Cambridge: Cambridge University Press.

Cooper, M. M. 1986: The ecology of writing. *College English*, 48, pp. 364–75.

Czerniewska, P. 1988: Objectives for language learning. In M. Jones and A. West (eds): *Learning Me Your Language*. London: Mary Glasgow, pp. 123–32.

Czerniewska, P. 1990: Reflecting on experience. In National Writing Project: *Ways of Looking*. Walton-on-Thames: Thomas Nelson, pp. 9–18.

DES (Department of Education and Science) 1975: *A Language for Life* (The Bullock Report). London: HMSO.

DES (Department of Education and Science) 1989: *English for Ages 5 to 16*. London: HMSO.

Dixon, J. 1967: *Growth through English*. London: Oxford University Press.

Donaldson, M. 1978: *Children's Minds*. London: Fontana.

Downing, J. and Leong, C. K. 1982: *Psychology of Reading*. New York: Macmillan.

Edwards, D. and Mercer, N. 1987: *Common Knowledge*. London: Methuen.

Elbow, P. 1973: *Writing without Teachers*. New York: Oxford University Press.

Faigley, L. 1986: Competing theories of process: a critique and a proposal. *College English*, 48, pp. 527–42.

Ferreiro, E. and Teberosky, A. 1982: *Literacy before Schooling*. London: Heinemann Educational.

Flower, L. and Hayes, J. R. 1980: A cognitive process theory of writing. *College Composition and Communication* 31, pp. 365–87.

Fox, C. 1983: Talking like a book. In M. Meek (ed.): *Opening Moves*. London: Bedford Way Papers.

Gee, J. P. 1986: Orality and literacy: from the savage mind to ways with words. *TESOL Quarterly*, 20, pp. 719–46.

Gee, J. P. 1987: What is literacy? *Teaching and Learning*, 2, pp. 3–11.

Gee, J. P. 1988: The legacies of literacy: from Plato to Freire through Harvey Graff. *Harvard Educational Review*, 58, pp. 195–212.

Gelb, I. J. 1963: *A Study of Writing*. Chicago: University of Chicago Press.

Gilbert, P. 1988: Authorship in the writing classroom: a critical comment. In S. De Castell, A. Luke and C. Luke (eds): *Language, Authority and Criticisms: Readings on the School Textbook*. Basingstoke: Falmer Press.

Goodman, Y. 1988: Writing development in young children. *Gnosis* 8.

Goody, J. 1977: *The Domestication of the Savage Mind*. Cambridge: Cambridge University Press.

Graves, D. 1981: Renters and owners: Donald Graves on writing. *The English Magazine*, 8, pp. 4–7.

Graves, D. 1983: *Writing: Teachers and Children at Work*. London: Heinemann Educational.

Green, B. 1987: Gender, genre and writing pedagogy. In I. Reid (ed.): *The Place of Genre in Learning: Current Debates*. Centre for Studies in Literary Education: Deakin University, Victoria, pp. 83–90.

Hall, N. 1987: *The Emergence of Literacy*. London: Hodder and Stoughton.

Halliday, M. A. K. 1985: *Spoken and Written Language*. Victoria: Deakin University Press.

Heath, S. B. 1982a: What no bedtime story means: narrative skills at home and school. *Language in Society*, 11, pp. 49–76.

Heath, S. B. 1982b: Protean shapes in literacy events: ever-shifting oral and literate traditions. In D. Tannen (ed.): *Spoken and Written Language*. Norwood, NJ: Ablex, pp. 91–117.

Heath, S. B. 1983: *Ways with Words: Language, Life and Work in Communities and Classrooms*. Cambridge: Cambridge University Press.

Hudson, R. 1983: The higher level differences between speech and writing. Unpublished paper presented at British Association of Applied Linguistics Conference.

Jensen, H. 1970: *Sign, Symbol and Script: an Account of Man's Efforts to Write*. London: Allen and Unwin.

Karmiloff-Smith, A. 1979: *A Functional Approach to Child Language*. Cambridge: Cambridge University Press.

Kress, G. 1982: *Learning to Write*. London: Routledge and Kegan Paul.

Maclure, M. 1986: Beginning writing: an interactional perspective. Paper presented to the Annual Meeting of the American Educational Research Association, San Francisco.

Martin, J. R. 1984: Types of writing in infants and primary school. *Proceedings of Macarthur Institute of Higher Education, Reading Language Symposium 5: Reading, Writing and Spelling*.

Martin, J. R., Christie, F. and Rothery, J. 1987: Social processes in education: a reply to Sawyer and Watson (and others). In I. Reid (ed.): *The Place of Genre in Learning: Current Debates*. Centre for Studies in Literary Education: Deakin University, Victoria, pp. 58–80.

Mercer, N. (ed.) 1981: *Language in Schools and Community*. London: Edward Arnold.

Mercer, N. (ed.) 1988: *Language and Literacy from an Educational Perspective.* Milton Keynes: Open University Press.

Michaels, S. 1981: 'Sharing time': children's narrative styles and differential access to literacy. *Language in Society*, 10, pp. 423–42.

Michaels, S. 1986: Narrative presentation: an oral preparation for literacy with first graders. In J. Cook-Gumperz (ed.): *The Social Construction of Literacy.* Cambridge: Cambridge University Press.

Murphy, J. *On the Way Home.* London: Macmillan.

Murray, D. 1984: *Write to Learn.* New York: Holt Rinehart Winston.

National Writing Project 1989a: *Becoming a Writer.* Walton-on-Thames: Thomas Nelson.

National Writing Project 1989b: *Writing and Learning.* Walton-on-Thames: Thomas Nelson.

National Writing Project 1989c: *Audiences for Writing.* Walton-on-Thames: Thomas Nelson.

National Writing Project 1990a: *Responding to and Assessing Writing.* Walton-on-Thames: Thomas Nelson.

National Writing Project 1990b: *Perceptions of Writing.* Walton-on-Thames: Thomas Nelson.

National Writing Project 1990c: *A Rich Resource: Writing and Language Diversity.* Walton-on-Thames: Thomas Nelson.

National Writing Project 1990d: *What Are Writers Made of? Issues of Gender and Writing.* Walton-on-Thames: Thomas Nelson.

National Writing Project 1990e: *Writing Partnerships (1): Home, School and Community.* Walton-on-Thames: Thomas Nelson.

National Writing Project 1990f: *Ways of Looking.* Walton-on-Thames: Thomas Nelson.

Olson, D. R., Torrance, N. and Hildyard, A. (eds) 1985: *Literacy, Language and Learning. The Nature and Consequences of Reading and Writing.* Cambridge: Cambridge University Press.

Perera, K. 1981: Some language problems in school learning. In N. Mercer (ed.): *Language in Schools and Community.* London: Edward Arnold.

Perera, K. 1984: *Children's Writing and Reading. Analysing Classroom Language.* Oxford: Blackwell.

Peters, M. L. 1985: *Spelling: Caught or Taught?* London: Routledge.

Reid, I. (ed.) 1987: *The Place of Genre in Learning: Current Debates.* Centre for Studies in Literary Education: Deakin University, Victoria.

Rothery, J. 1984: The development of genres – primary to junior secondary school. In *Deakin University Course Study Guide: Children Writing.* Victoria: Deakin University.

Rowe, C. J. 1986: *Plato: Phaedrus* (translation and commentary). Warminster, Wilts: Aris and Philips.

Saussure, F. de 1916: *Cours de Linguistique Générale*, 5th edn. Paris: Payot. (English translation by W. Baskin, 1959: *Course in General Linguistics*. New York: McGraw Hill.)

Scollon, R. and Scollon, S. B. K. 1981: *Narrative, Literacy and Face in Interethnic Communication*. Norwood, NJ: Ablex.

Scragg, D. G. 1974: *A History of English Spelling*. Manchester: Manchester University Press.

Scribner, S. and Cole, M. 1981: *The Psychology of Literacy*. Cambridge: Harvard University Press.

Scribner, S. and Cole, M. 1988: Unpackaging literacy. In N. Mercer (ed.): *Language and Literacy from an Educational Perspective*, vol. 1. Milton Keynes: Open University Press, pp. 241–55.

Spencer, M. 1986: Emergent literacies: a site for analysis. *Language Arts*, 63, pp. 442–53.

Street, B. 1984: *Literacy in Theory and Practice*. Cambridge: Cambridge University Press.

Stubbs, M. 1980: *Language and Literacy*. London: Routledge and Kegan Paul.

Tannen, D. 1985: Relative focus on involvement in oral and written discourse. In D. R. Olson, N. Torrance and A. Hildyard (eds): *Literacy, Language and Learning. The Nature and Consequences of Reading and Writing*. Cambridge: Cambridge University Press, pp. 124–47.

Teale, W. H. and Sulzby, E. 1988: Emergent literacy as a perspective for examining how young children become writers and readers. In N. Mercer (ed.): *Language and Literacy from an Educational Perspective*, vol. 1. Milton Keynes: Open University Press, pp. 256–62.

Temple, C. A., Nathan, R. G. and Burris, N. A. 1982: *The Beginnings of Writing*. Boston: Allyn and Bacon.

Vygotsky, L. S. 1978: *Mind in Society*. Cambridge: Harvard University Press.

Wade, B. 1983: Getting it together: the value of story in language development. *Cambridge Journal of Education*, 13.

White, J. 1985: Writing on the wall. Unpublished paper presented at the British Educational Research Association Conference, University of Sheffield.

White, J. 1986: Writing and gender. Unpublished paper presented at the National Writing Project Coordinators' Seminar, Wakefield.

White, J. (in collaboration with Welford, G.) 1987: *The Language of*

Science: Making and Interpreting Observations. Report prepared for the Assessment of Performance Unit, Department of Education and Science.

White, J. 1989: *Pupils' Attitudes to Writing*. Report prepared for the Assessment of Performance Unit, Department of Education and Science. London: HMSO.

White, J. 1990: Questions of choice and change. In National Writing Project: *What Are Writers Made of? Issues of Gender*. Walton-on-Thames: Thomas Nelson, pp. 49–59.

Index